D1630043

THE OFFICIAL
WARRINGTON
WOLVES
MISCELLANY

GARY SLATER

The
History
Press

*To Warrington fans: who know how to
celebrate victory and defeat*

First published in 2012 by

The History Press
The Mill, Brimscombe Port
Stroud, Gloucestershire, GL5 2QG
www.thehistorypress.co.uk

British Library Cataloguing in Publication Data.
A catalogue record for this book is available from the British Library.

ISBN 978 0 7524 6472 5

Typesetting and origination by The History Press
Printed in Great Britain

ACKNOWLEDGEMENTS

Lee Briers, a great player and a great bloke, wrote a fascinating foreword which I am sure you will enjoy. Eddie Fuller set up and took the photograph of Lee on the front cover, much to his embarrassment, and has now been the club photographer for an incredible 40 seasons. Thanks also to Stan Lewandowski of the Warrington Wolves Past Players' Association; Mike Parsons and his team at the *Warrington Guardian*; Neil Dowson and Andy Topham at the Warrington Wolves and everyone who knows me. Neil read and corrected the original manuscript while another Neil, Neil Ormston, helped with the statistics. Here's to many more seasons in the sun.

FOREWORD

That's me in the middle on the front cover after breaking Steve Hesford's points-scoring record against Swinton in May last year. All the fuss was a bit embarrassing to be honest and I didn't really want to be carried by Moz (Adrian Morley) and Garreth Carvell but they made it a special occasion and it is one of the things I will look back on when I finish my career and think, 'wow, that was pretty good.'

Going into the game I knew I was close to the record, I think I needed 35 points, but I didn't believe for one minute that I was going to break it in that one game and score 44 points. I just thought that I would knock off as many points as I could. It was a shame for Swinton, who lost 112–0, but their players never gave up and kept going right to the end. We spoke to the Swinton guys afterwards and told them not to get too downhearted because we were putting big scores on Super League sides at the time.

Moz and Garreth are brilliant props. Moz's record speaks for itself. He has been around a long time and played on both sides of the world and Garreth has come into some great form after being underrated. In fact, all the pack we have now make my job much easier. I've been blessed with good half-back partners as well – Allan Langer, Andrew Johns, Nat Wood, Richie Myler and Michael Monaghan have all been a joy to play with.

Nat was the funniest player I've played with. He was a real prankster and he loved to play tricks on people. He is back in Australia now, running his own business and doing very well and we still keep in touch. He was responsible for the funniest moment I've had at Warrington when he scored that try against Wigan at The Halliwell Jones Stadium in 2004 and ran through the stand. That was bizarre but it was quite funny and apparently he asked a Wigan fan for a bite of his hot dog on the way.

Winning the Carnegie Challenge Cup at Wembley against Huddersfield Giants in 2009 and Leeds Rhinos in 2010 was special for everyone involved. Against Leeds, I collected the Lance Todd Trophy as man of the match which was a bonus for myself, but you win cups as a team. I was lucky enough to be the man of the match but you don't win finals without everybody playing really well.

Tony Smith, the Warrington coach, has made a big difference. His man-management is fantastic. He treats every player differently and knows how to get the best out of them. He also comes from a successful background, with Leeds and Huddersfield. He knows how to win and has given us that belief.

I have won things late on in my professional career and my amateur career with St Helens Crusaders was the same. It was only at under-15s and under-16s that we started winning trophies. It was a strange old weekend when I joined Warrington in 1997. I signed on the Friday and then went back to my hometown club St Helens on the Sunday and we got a pasting but I have never once regretted signing for Warrington and I think that is the main thing. I have enjoyed every minute of it and long may that continue.

Rugby league has taken me all over the world, to Scotland, Wales, France, Australia and New Zealand, and I've met people of different nationalities, beliefs and faiths and it is not often that you meet a bad person in the game. All the players are really good blokes and enjoy the camaraderie. I have been all over the world playing for Warrington and there aren't many jobs you can do that in.

I've also been to the House of Lords for the All-Party Parliamentary Rugby League Group annual dinner and that was a brilliant day too. Paul Cullen and I were shown all around parliament and at one point Margaret Thatcher was sat literally ten metres away from us. Then we had dinner and I received the group's player of the year award. It was a great day and I really enjoyed it. It was a shame we were playing a couple of days later because it would have been nice to get a few cheap drinks in. I couldn't believe how cheap their ale was!

All the way through school, all I ever wanted to do was be a professional rugby league player and my school work took second place unfortunately – I regret that a bit now but I always wanted to be a rugby player.

My advice to young players today would be to enjoy it, learn as much as you can and listen to your coaches and if you do that you won't be far off. I want to go into coaching myself but not for a few years yet. I am having too much fun playing. Enjoy the book.

Lee Briers, Warrington's record points-scorer, 2012

GREATEST VICTORY

23 August 2000, 7–4

Warrington Wolves' most important victory was not achieved on the pitch, on the training ground or at Red Hall in Leeds, the headquarters of the Rugby Football League. It happened in the council chamber when Warrington Borough Council's planning committee voted 7–4 in favour of the club's application to build a new ground, in partnership with Tesco, on the site of the former Tetley Walker brewery.

That vote was not the end of the process – it led to a public inquiry the following May – but without it there would not have been a new stadium. In the build-up to the planning committee meeting, the club staged an emotional question and answer session at the Parr Hall on 17 July 2000, showing a virtual reality video of the new ground.

The late Peter Deakin, who was the club's chief executive at the time, also wrote to all season-ticket holders, 'I cannot underestimate the importance of a new stadium to the future of the club. It is only with the creation of the People's Stadium that the club will be able to satisfy Super League's impending facility requirements and develop the revenue streams to allow the Wolves to realise our potential as a top level Super League club.'

A decade on, following back-to-back Challenge Cup wins in 2009 and 2010, the outstanding success of The Halliwell Jones Stadium is there for all to see.

THE HALLIWELL JONES STADIUM

A colleague in London once asked me if Halliwell Jones was a former Warrington player, perhaps a Welsh scrum-half from the 1960s? The truth, of course, is that Halliwell Jones is an authorised BMW and Mini dealer which agreed a 10-year deal for the naming rights of the stadium. In May 2011, Halliwell

Jones signed a 6-year extension to that contract until 2017. The stadium and the accompanying Tesco Extra store were built by Barr Construction. It took them just 43 weeks to build the stadium at a cost of £8 million. Work started on 9 December 2002 and was completed on 6 October 2003.

The North Stand is the main stand and is all-seater, with a capacity of 3,200. The East Stand (the Martin Dawes Stand) is also all-seater, with a capacity of 2,398. The South Stand (The Halliwell Jones Stand) is a standing terrace with a capacity of 4,000. Finally, the West Stand (the Doodson Stand) is also a standing terrace, with a capacity of 3,200. There are 226 disabled and carer places.

The pitch is the maximum size allowed (120 metres by 74 metres) with a 3-metre run-off. The stadium has five changing rooms, for home and away first teams, home and away academy teams and one for the officials. The stadium has been a no smoking venue since 1 January 2006 following a poll of supporters when 63 per cent voted for the measure.

GETTING SHIRTY

When Warrington Wolves played Castleford Tigers at The Halliwell Jones Stadium in May 2011, they wore a special camouflage kit to mark the club's Armed Forces Day. The club donated £5 from every replica camouflage kit sold to charity – namely Help for Heroes and the Mercian Regiment Benevolent Fund. The camouflage certainly fooled Castleford as Warrington won 62–0. A generation earlier, in September 1987, Warrington forgot to take their kit to Castleford for a league game and had to borrow a reserve strip from the home team. The change of colours did not seem to do them any harm, on that occasion either, as Warrington won 40–30. Warrington made a special kit for their match against Australia in November 1994 but the Rugby Football League ruled that they could not play in it. Some supporters still bought it, however, and proudly wear it to this day.

THAT'S ENTERTAINMENT

Super League and summer rugby brought about a new era in pre-match entertainment, including the Starlites, a sensational dancing ensemble, although not every supporting act was as well received. Irish twins Jedward, fresh from *X-Factor*, were booed off at The Halliwell Jones Stadium before the Harlequins match in February 2010. For fans of a certain age, however, the most memorable pre-match music is 'Entry of the Gladiators' by Julius Fucik, which still evokes memories of Brian Bevan and the boys trotting out on to the Wilderspool pitch.

MONEY, MONEY, MONEY

From the 1880s onwards, Warrington have been paying their players and quite right too. The players – to use a modern expression – put their bodies on the line for the club and deserve to be rewarded for their time and commitment. Forward Will Randles played for Warrington in the late 1880s and early 1890s and then trained the team for 7 years. He said that in his day winning pay was two tuppenny vouchers worth two gills of ale while losing pay was just one tuppenny voucher for one gill of ale. This beer money was soon replaced by the real thing. In 1895/96, rugby league's first season as the Northern Union, players were limited to a 'broken time payment' of *6s* a day. 'Broken time payments' were made in lieu of work, so players had to have a full-time job, otherwise they couldn't play. This wasn't a game for slackers, ne'er-do-wells or, worst of all, professionals. In today's money, that *6s* a day is the equivalent of £100.

THINGS THEY SAID

'It's a girl – and I'm playing.'

Paul Wood's message to Tony Smith after his wife gave birth to a daughter on the morning of the match against Crusaders in 2011 – he played and scored two tries

'Alex Murphy got sent off and one of the Castleford lads tried to break my ribs.'

John Bevan recalls his debut in September 1973

'It wasn't the same as Warrington. We even had to wash our own kit!'

Brian Glover on his move to St Helens in 1970

'I find myself watching him to such an extent that I forget that I'm on the field too.'

Albert Johnson on Brian Bevan

'I have a wife and child, and I am only a working man. I was offered £100 down, and I couldn't resist it.'

Billy O'Neill after signing for Warrington from Cardiff in October 1908

'If Brian Bevan had been a cricketer he would have been knighted. If he'd been a soccer player he'd have got the OBE. If he'd been an actor he'd have got an Oscar.'

Oscar-winner Colin Welland

'My signing-on fee was a small lemonade, a cigar and a pat on the back – and I didn't even smoke!'

Ernie Brookes (1902–20) on signing for Warrington

'The Warrington spectators are the worst spectators in England.'

Batley's Welsh winger, Wattie Davies, after being sent off at Wilderspool in September 1901

'My attitude was "get your retaliation in first" and I wasn't the only player like that in those days.'

Joe Price explains the laws of the jungle in the 1960s and '70s

'He always wore the same socks. Well he played for 20 years so it wasn't the same socks for 20 years, but you know what I mean.'

Jeanette Lane, Brian Bevan's daughter, in 2008

'He came back from his honeymoon twice to go training.'

Jeanette Lane again, in 2008

'If you didn't win, you didn't eat.'

Paul Cullen, recalling the days of winning pay and losing pay, 1999

'Let's hope Brett Hodgson gets back into the team quickly otherwise my goal-kicking record will be gone as well.'

Steve Hesford in 2011 after Lee Briers had broken his club points-scoring record

'I didn't see his face but I would recognise the boot anywhere.'

Ray Price after being kicked in the head by a supporter during a fracas in the 1954 GB tour of Australia

RECORD BUYS

£100: Warrington paid £100 to the Wales international forward Billy O'Neill when they signed him from Cardiff in October 1908.

£700: Warrington paid St Helens £700 in September 1934 to sign their international forward Jack Arkwright.

£1,450: Warrington paid Liverpool Stanley a world record £1,450 to sign their international full-back Billy Belshaw in October 1937. Warrington also agreed to find a job for his dad, something that was not publicised at the time.

£4,600: Warrington paid Widnes a world record £4,600 to sign their Lancashire centre Albert Naughton in November 1949. St Helens, in fact, offered £5,000 but Naughton, quite understandably, wanted to come to Warrington.

£12,500: Warrington paid Leigh £12,500 in August 1971 for forwards Geoff Clarkson and Dave Chisnall. Chisnall was valued at £8,000.

£75,000: Warrington signed Widnes scrum-half Andy Gregory in January 1985 in a 'world record' £75,000 deal. Widnes received Warrington's £70,000 transfer-listed forward John Fieldhouse plus a 'substantial' cash sum. The transfer was not recognised as a world record deal because it was not cash only.

£200,000: Warrington paid St Helens £200,000 in July 2004 for Great Britain centre Martin Gleeson, even though he was serving a four-month ban at the time for betting against his own team.

£290,000: Warrington paid Salford City Reds £215,000 up front for England scrum-half Richie Myler in September 2009 with a further £75,000 to follow as various targets were reached. It was a record fee for a teenager (he was still only 19) and a record fee for a scrum-half.

RECORD SALES

£9,500: Warrington received £9,500 from Wigan for forward Laurie Gilfedder in August 1963.

£40,000: Warrington received £40,000 from Wigan for Ford in February 1985 – a then record fee for a winger.

£130,000: Warrington received £130,000 from Wigan for scrum-half Andy Gregory in January 1987. Gregory had been transfer-listed at £150,000 but that figure had been reduced to £130,000 after he appealed to the Rugby Football League.

£350,000: Warrington had transfer-listed 20-year-old Iestyn Harris at a world record £1,350,000 in July 1996 after he fell out with the club. He was eventually sold to Leeds Rhinos the following April with Warrington receiving £325,000 plus teenage prop Danny Sculthorpe.

£370,000: Warrington sold captain Paul Sculthorpe to St Helens in December 1997 for £370,000 – a world record fee for a forward. Warrington received £300,000 in cash plus the £70,000-rated Chris Morley.

FOUNDING FATHERS

The club that became Warrington Wolves was founded in the summer of 1876 by seven young men – the so-called 'Founding Fathers' – at a meeting at St Paul's Church Sunday School on Bewsey Road, Warrington.

St Paul's was a Church of England church and was built in 1830, closed in 1980 and has since been demolished and replaced by an old people's home, although the church graveyard still remains. Coincidentally, St Paul's was just 400 metres away from the spot on Winwick Road where The Halliwell Jones Stadium can be found.

The seven young men, all aged about 20, were William Henry Wallington, his brother Thomas Wallington, G.J. Browne, G.W. Edwards, Earnest Early, Ebenezer England and Thomas Rathbone. William Wallington worked for Warrington Council (Warrington Corporation as it was known at the time), rising to become the markets superintendent and inspector of weights and measures.

G.J. Browne became a director of the boatbuilders Messrs Clare and Ridgway who had a boatyard at Sankey Bridges and launched their boats, sideways, into Sankey Canal until 1913. G.W. Edwards became a solicitor in Liverpool while Earnest Early was a railway clerk with the London & North Western Railway and the first club captain but had to give up the role after three months when the railway transferred him to another district. Ebenezer England lived to the grand old age of 81 and was still a keen supporter of the club right up to his death in March 1939. England was a member of Warrington Rural Council, representing Poulton-with-Fearnhead, and served on Padgate Parish Council.

For reasons which are still unclear, the club these seven young men founded was called Warrington Zingari. Zingari is the Italian word for gypsies and so a zingari club was a wandering or nomadic team.

Warrington Zingari's first game was played at Wharf Meadow but any record of it has been lost in the mists of time. The first match we still know about was against nearby Penketh at Penketh on Saturday 28 October 1876 and Warrington lost by one goal, one try and two touchdowns to nil. Things could only get better.

Confusingly, tries and touchdowns were different things. Tries were scored when a player crossed the try line with the ball in his hands. Touchdowns were scored when the ball was kicked over the try line and a player touched it down.

The Warrington team against Penketh was T. Rathbone, F. Monks, W. Edwards, T. Wallington, H. Maybury, P. Whittle, J. Massey, J. Sutton and S. Sutton, who were all forwards; W. Wallington (captain), T. Howard, G.J. Browne, R. Andrews, D. Brinsley and J. Gaskell, who were all backs.

AROUND THE GROUNDS

Warrington Wolves have had nine home grounds. The first was the romantically named Wharf Meadow on Wharf Street, Warrington, which is now home to the Riverside Retail Park. Warrington only played there for one season before hopping back and forth across the town in search of a permanent home. The full list of the club's grounds is as follows:

Season	Ground
1876/77	Wharf Meadow, Wharf Street
1877/78 and 1878/79	Arpley (near the cricket ground)
1879/80	Sankey Street (*Warrington Guardian* site)
1880/81	Wilderspool Road
1881/82	Slutchers Lane
1882/83	Sankey Street (behind the post office)
1883/84 to 1897/98	Wilderspool Road
1898/99–2003	Wilderspool Stadium
2004 onwards	The Halliwell Jones Stadium

The two Wilderspool Road grounds and Wilderspool Stadium took their names from the nearby Wilderspool Causeway. Wilderspool means 'wild beasts' pool' and that perhaps explains all the animal aggression that was seen on the grounds. In the 1980s, opposition players (notably those from Wigan) started to call Wilderspool 'the zoo' because of Warrington's fierce pack of forwards: Les Boyd, Kevin Tamati, Bob Jackson, Alan Rathbone and friends. Peter Higham, the Warrington chairman at the time, once joked that he had decided to sign so many rough, tough and uncompromising forwards because it was unlikely that they would all feature in the same side – one or more would always be suspended.

Talking of wild beasts, there were plans to parade Simba – an 11-year-old lion – around Wilderspool before the Wales versus England game in September 1975, but the idea was abandoned after talks with the police. Warrington were led out on to the pitch by a ram, the Mercian Regiment's mascot, for the Super League match against Castleford in May 2011. The ram, flanked by two officers, was wearing a primrose and blue scarf around his neck.

THE 100 TRY CLUB

More than 1,000 men have played for Warrington since rugby league was born in 1895, but only 17 of them have scored 100 tries for the first team. The first was winger Jack Fish who achieved the feat in the 1905 Challenge Cup final against Hull KR at Headingley. The full list is as follows:

1	Brian Bevan (1945–62)	740
2	Jack Fish (1898–1911)	214
3	John Bevan (1973–86)	201
4	Mark Forster (1983–2000)	191
5=	Parry Gordon (1963–81)	167
5=	Albert Naughton (1949–61)	167
7	Billy Dingsdale (1928–40)	154
8	Lee Briers (1997–)	144
9	Bobby Greenough (1957–66)	136
10	Jim Challinor (1952–63)	135
11	Brian Glover (1957–70)	130
12	Jim Tranter (1911–28)	120
13	Bob Eccles (1977–87)	119
14=	Tommy Thompson (1927–34)	112
14=	Albert Johnson (1939–51)	112
16	Gerry Helme (1945–57)	101
17	Lee Penny (1992–2003)	100

From the birth of rugby league in 1895 until the end of the 1982/83 season tries were worth 3 points. From the start of the 1983/84 campaign their value was increased to 4 points in an attempt to reward attacking play. Centre Paul Cullen was the last Warrington player to score a 3-point try, in the closing minutes of a 32–13 victory over Workington Town at Wilderspool in April 1983. Winger Paul Fellows was the first Warrington player to score a 4-pointer in a 22–22 draw at Hull that August.

PLAYER OF THE 1880S – TOMMY BARNES

Tommy Barnes was Warrington's first great player and was a three-quarter in the days when there were only three three-quarters. His finest hour in a Warrington shirt came in the 1886 West Lancashire and Border Towns Union Cup final against Aspull when he kicked the winning dropped goal to give the Wirepullers their first trophy. The following season he scored 12 tries and kicked 3 goals and 8 dropped goals which was said to be the best return by any player in England. After that he was elected captain for the 1887/88 campaign – and I really do mean elected. He polled 86 votes, way ahead of his nearest challengers, Will Dillon (23) and Fair Turner (7). A local lad, Barnes had made his debut, aged 16, in 1881 and quickly became the team's match-winner. After he had kicked the winning dropped goal against Widnes in March 1886, some supporters carried him on their shoulders from the Wilderspool Road ground through the town to the Griffin Hotel in Horsemarket Street so that they could buy him a drink. That same season the club even paid him when he was injured, a fact that would have appalled the Rugby Football Union (had they known about it) but which showed what an important player he was to the team. When he died in 1926, aged 60, the club flag flew at half mast at Wilderspool as a mark of respect.

Honours: West Lancashire and Border Towns Union Cup 1885/86

FIRST FIXTURE LIST

Warrington's oldest surviving fixture list dates from the 1877/78 season. Warrington would play 10 teams home and away before the end of March as follows:

13 October	Chester	H
20 October	Newton Heath	H
27 October	Cheetham Hill	A
3 November	Runcorn	A
10 November	Lowton	A
17 November	Crewe	H
1 December	Lymm	H
8 December	Urmston	A
15 December	West Leigh	H
22 December	Chester	A
29 December	Cheetham Hill	H
5 January	Newton Heath	A
12 January	Runcorn	H
19 January	Widnes	H
26 January	Lowton	H
2 February	Crewe	A
16 February	Lymm	A
23 February	Urmston	H
2 March	West Leigh	A
9 March	Widnes	A

MOTLEY CREWE

In the early days of rugby there were no referees, with each side supplying an umpire instead. This inevitably led to problems – as at Crewe in February 1878. Warrington lost heavily, but that tells only half of the story. Three minutes from time one of the Crewe men ran behind the Warrington goal line and claimed a try. The Crewe umpire allowed it but the Warrington umpire ruled that the player was off-side – hence it was recorded as a disputed try. By now, however, the Warrington players and umpire had had enough and left the field.

The Crewe supporters were not amused and, according to the *Warrington Evening Post*, 'commenced hooting and yelling in a most hideous fashion.' The Warrington players were, 'pelted in fine style with cabbage stalks, our umpire especially seemed to be a favourite, as he came in for far more than his fair share. We just mention these facts so that clubs who have fixtures with the Crewe St George FC may know what sort of reception they may expect when they visit that town, unless they are prepared to submit to everything which those gentlemen may require at their hands.'

There are, of course, always two sides to every story and a Mr F. Smith, the honorary secretary of Crewe St George's, wrote to the *Warrington Evening Post* a few days later. He accused Warrington players of shouting 'break his legs' when beaten by an opponent. He also dismissed the claim that cabbage stalks had been thrown, saying that only 'an old shoe' was thrown by a youth.

SPRINTING TO WARRINGTON

In rugby, as the old saying goes, there is no substitute for pace. So, in their time, Warrington have signed two Olympic sprinters to play on the wing. Mateaki Mafi (1995–7) had represented Tonga, aged 19, in the 200 metres at the 1992 Barcelona Games, finishing fifth in his heat. His best time for the 100 metres was 10.3 seconds.

Ted Haggis ran in the 100 metres for Canada at the 1948 London Games, finishing second in his heat in a time of 10.9 seconds to reach the quarter-finals. He signed for Warrington in January 1950, causing great excitement in the town. More than 6,000 people turned up at Wilderspool to see him make his debut on the left wing for Warrington 'A' against Lancashire Amateurs and Haggis rewarded the fans by scoring a try. However, he never made the quantum leap from top-class athletics to top-class rugby league and, after half a dozen 'A' team outings, he returned home to Ontario, having enjoyed the experience immensely.

LEAGUE OF NATIONS

More than 100 overseas players have played for Warrington's first team. The total is made up of 58 Australians, 39 New Zealanders and the following fellow travellers:

Fiji	Manoa Thompson
France	Jerome Guisset
Morocco	Hussein M'Barki
Papua New Guinea	Tom O'Reilly, John Wilshere
Samoa	Danny Lima, Willie Swann, Tony Tatupu
South Africa	Toby du Toit
Tonga	Salesi Finau, Mateaki Mafi
USA	Taylor Welch

GREAT SCOTS

In 1997 scrum-half John Duffy became the first Warrington player to represent Scotland. The club has had three other

Bravehearts – full-back Lee Penny, winger Jason Roach and loose-forward Mike Wainwright. All three made their debuts in 1998.

AN IRELAND RACE

In 1997 winger Mark Forster became the first Warrington player to represent Ireland, thanks to an Irish grandmother, and won 8 caps, scoring 4 tries. The club has had six other Wolfhounds: Chris Bridge, Ben Harrison, Dean Gaskell, Tyrone McCarthy, Rob Smyth and Simon Grix. Bridge and Harrison have since switched their allegiance to England.

ENGLAND, WALES AND GREAT BRITAIN

Warrington have had 51 England internationals, 36 Wales internationals and 52 Great Britain internationals. In other words, too many to list in a miscellany, but honourable mentions must be made to players who have captained their country. Billy Belshaw and Adrian Morley have led England, Jonathan Davies and Lee Briers have captained Wales and Eric Fraser, Mike Gregory and Morley have led the Lions. In the 2011 Gillette Four Nations final, Morley also became the first player to win 50 Great Britain/England caps. His total was made up of 30 GB caps and 20 England caps.

WORLD CUP WINNERS

1954   Albert Naughton, Gerry Helme
1960   Jim Challinor, Eric Fraser, Bobby Greenough
1988   Steve Roach (Australia)

BIG BANS

Warrington stand-off Mel de Lloyd was banned sine die (indefinitely) while guesting for Keighley in January 1942. In a game at Hull, de Lloyd was sent off for disputing a decision and then hit the referee so he could have few complaints. The suspension was lifted 11 months later. Forward Joe Price was banned for 11 months for a high tackle on St Helens' Graham Liptrot in January 1974. The suspension was reduced to 4 months on appeal but still meant that he missed out on Wembley as well as the Player's No. 6 Trophy and Club Championship finals.

LET THERE BE LIGHT

Warrington played their first match under floodlights against Widnes on Friday 15 November 1878. The following day's *Warrington Evening Post* takes up the story under the snappy headline, 'Football Match By Electric Light At Warrington'.

Last night, according to announcement, a football match was played on Arpley cricket ground by the electric light, which is just now creating so much sensation in scientific circles, and amongst the public in general. The lamps were placed, one on the town end of the ground, and the other at the extreme portion of the field near the Bowling Green. The weather, during the latter part of the match, got worse rather than better, rain falling heavily. The game was finished about half past eight, Widnes winning by one goal, four tries and four touchdowns, to Warrington's one touchdown.

More than 85 years later floodlit rugby league finally came to Wilderspool when, on Tuesday 28 September 1965, the club's original lights were switched on by John Whitley, managing director of brewers Greenall Whitley, who had helped to pay for them. To mark the occasion, the Wire played Wigan in a floodlit friendly and produced one of their best displays of the season to win 9–5.

Suitably equipped, Wilderspool was chosen to stage the first game in the new BBC2 Floodlit Trophy in October 1965. Widnes were the visitors and won 20–10 in front of the cameras, although the game was only screened in the south of England so as not to reduce the attendance.

The floodlights failed in the league match against Halifax at Wilderspool on Monday 18 October 1993. The scores were tied at 6–6 after 9 minutes of the second half when the lights went out – shortly after Jonathan Davies had knocked on – and the players had to leave the field. Ground announcer Peter Robinson jokingly put out an appeal for an electrician while his assistant, Phil Shaw, played 'Always Look on the Bright Side of Life'. After a 24-minute delay, the lights came back on and Davies won the match for Warrington with a thrilling kick-and-chase try, 2 penalties and a drop goal to make the final score 15–7. The game ended at 10.04 p.m., the latest finish in the club's history.

SPORTS DAY

Warrington staged their first annual athletic festival and gala at the end of the 1883/84 season. It quickly became a popular fund-raising event and was switched to August as an introduction to the season, attracting thousands of spectators. The most famous sports day was held at Wilderspool on Bank Holiday Monday 4 August 1902 and attracted a crowd of 8,000. The fans' favourite, winger Jack Fish, won the 100 yards and 220 yards sprint handicap races. His prize for winning the 100 yards was a magnificent carved oak bracket chime clock worth £10, about £800 in today's money. Warrington's other famous winger of the day, Elliot Harris, won the 440 yards title. He had more sense than to take on Fish.

TALKING TURNSTILES

Warrington's early grounds were little more than fields with a fence around them and an attendant on duty at the entrance for supporters to contribute what they could afford. The players got changed in a local pub, such as the Patten Arms or the White Hart, and then walked to the ground. It was not a foolproof system for collecting funds as one story from the 1880s demonstrates. Warrington, who were based at the White Hart at the time, were at home to Runcorn, who were one of the leading teams, and a gate of 2,000 was anticipated. The attendant collected some money from supporters but then disappeared, allowing the rest in for free. He was later discovered propping up the bar in the White Hart, nursing a pint pot and a hangover. As attendances continued to rise, Warrington first installed turnstiles at their Wilderspool Road ground in October 1887. The Halliwell Jones Stadium currently has 24 turnstiles and they are linked to a computerised counting system in the control room.

DEATH BY MISADVENTURE

Another home game against Runcorn, at Sankey Street on Saturday 10 January 1880, ended in tragedy. The teams had been playing for about 45 minutes when Alfred Whitehead, one of the Warrington three-quarters, set off on a run. He beat several men but was then stopped in his tracks by 22-year-old Alfred Bibby, a sailmaker from Widnes, who butted him on the thigh and whose head then hit the ground.

Whitehead, the stronger and heavier man, was hurt and started limping, but Bibby was in a bad way and lay unconscious on the ground. Brandy was administered and a doctor was sent for. The doctor examined Bibby and ordered that he be taken to Warrington Infirmary where he died

6 minutes after admission. The *Warrington Guardian* reported that, 'The melancholy accident cast quite a gloom over the town when it became known that Bibby was dead.'

An inquest was held at the White Hart (where the two teams would have got changed) two days later and heard evidence from Whitehead and another Warrington player, Ebenezer England, one of the Founding Fathers. The inquest was told that Bibby had died of 'compression of the brain' and the inquest jury returned a verdict of 'death by misadventure'.

DIAL M FOR MERGER

When the Super League was created in April 1995, there was a major catch: Warrington and Widnes were supposed to merge to form a Cheshire club. There was outrage in both towns and a 'Save the Wire' campaign was launched, leading to the idea being dropped. There had, however, been two successful mergers in the club's early years. First, before the start of the 1881/82 season, Warrington merged with the Padgate Excelsior club. The amalgamation gave Warrington a motto, 'Excelsior!', which remained in vogue until the Second World War. Secondly, before the start of the 1884/85 season, they merged with Warrington Wanderers. Both mergers gave the club, now known as Warrington Football Club, extra players and prestige.

The amalgamation with Padgate was the most important, although it did not provide the club with extra funds, as former player David Tinnion explained in a speech in September 1903, 'In 1881/82 the Padgate club had a balance of £2 10s in hand but they were a very good set of fellows and, thinking they were giving Warrington enough in their talent, they decided to spend the balance on a dinner, and a jolly good dinner they had.'

In today's money £2 10s is worth about £500. Tinnion continued, 'The Warrington Football Club at that time were not in quite such good feather and in such excellent clover. The only thing they possessed was a slight balance against them, some goal posts, a few jerseys and a worn-out football.'

PLAYER OF THE 1890s – FAIR BARBER (1893–7)

Thomas Fairclough Barber (to give him his full name) was Warrington's captain in the 1895/96 season, the first following the breakaway from the Rugby Football Union to form the Northern Union, at the age of just 20. Also that season, he played 3 times for Lancashire, scoring on his debut, to help the Red Rose county win the inaugural rugby league County Championship. Fair was a flying winger who had joined the Wirepullers in 1893 after the Stockton Heath club disbanded and scored a try on his debut against Rugby that December. After that he never looked back, becoming a regular try-scorer and goal-kicker until his career was ended prematurely by injury in 1898. After his playing days were over he was elected on to the committee and later became club president. In August 1925, as club president, he officially opened an extension to the main stand before the game against Batley. A crowd of 9,000 was there to witness the occasion and cheer Warrington to a 13–2 victory. He died after a long illness, aged 58, in April 1933, just days before the club's first Wembley final.

Rugby league appearances: 70
Tries: 13
Goals: 17
Points: 76

FIRST TROPHY

Warrington won their first trophy, the West Lancashire and Border Towns Union Cup, by beating Aspull by 9 points to 1 in the final in April 1886. The match was held on the cricket ground of the Liverpool College, Fairfield, and attracted a crowd of between 5,000 and 6,000. Tommy Barnes kicked the winning dropped goal, then worth 6 points.

The Warrington team was as follows: Jimmy Buxton, full-back; Jim Jolley, Tommy Barnes and H. Boardman, three-quarter backs; Ned Gilbert and Will Speakman, half-backs; Fair (short for Fairfield) Turner, Frank Turner, Will Dillon, Ned Dillon, Tony Davies, Walter Povey, J. Rigby, Harry Ashton (captain) and William Hayes, forwards.

The team arrived back at Central station at 8.15 p.m. to be greeted by a large crowd and two brass bands. Players and officials, including club president Councillor Richard Francomb, took their seats in a wagonette drawn by four horses and set off in procession along Horsemarket Street, Sankey Street, Parker Street, Wilson Patten Street, Bridge Street, Buttermarket Street, Scotland Road and then back to the club's headquarters, the Griffin Hotel in Horsemarket Street, where toasts were proposed.

'The customary drink from the cup was then enjoyed, and several short complimentary speeches were delivered,' reported the *Warrington Guardian*. 'The remainder of the evening was spent at the hotel, and the proceedings were enlivened by music and singing.'

Ten days later, on Tuesday 20 April, a public banquet in recognition of the victory was held at the Lion Hotel on Bridge Street where there were more speeches and celebrating. The Griffin Hotel has since been demolished and a branch of the Royal Bank of Scotland now stands on the site.

BROTHERS IN ARMS

Warrington's first cup-winning team (see page 27) contained two sets of brothers – Fair and Frank Turner and Will and Ned Dillon – to set a pattern that continues to this day. Among the many sets of brothers to have played for the club are:

Louis and Vinnie Anderson (Challenge Cup winners in 2009 and 2010)
James and Bob Bate (1890s)
Brian and Owen Bevan (1940s and '50s)
Alf and Peter Boardman (1900s)
Brian and Jim Brady (1970s)
Barry and Wilf Briggs (1970s)
Billy and Tommy Cunliffe (1920s)
Martin and Tom Dickens (1960s and '70s)
Ben and Billy Dingsdale (1920s)
Ian and Ronnie Duane (1980s)
Bobby and Jackie Edwards (1960s)
Ben and Rhys Evans (2010s) – twins
Harry and Jack Garrett (1930s)
Mark and Martin Gleeson (2000s)
Chris and David Highton (1990s)
Leo and Ray Hindle (1940s)
Michael and Joel Monaghan (2010s)
Albert and Danny Naughton (1950s)
Barry and Steve Peters (1980s)
Barry and Mike Philbin (Challenge Cup winners in 1974)
Arthur and John Skelhorn (1920s)
Anthony and Willie Swann (1990s)
Ged and Jack Waring (1940s and '50s)

Keeping it in the family, Joe and Peter O'Toole and George and Duane Mann were cousins. Logan Swann was the cousin of Anthony and Willie Swann.

GENERATION GAME

Among the many fathers and sons who have played for Warrington are the following:

Father	Son
Jack Arkwright	Jack Arkwright
Dave Cotton	Dave Cotton
Jack Garrett	Wilf Garrett
Keith Holden	Keith Holden
Jack Jenkins	Griff Jenkins
Les Perkins	Ray Perkins
Roy Pickersgill	Steve Pickersgill
Freddie Ryder	Ron Ryder
Mal Thomas	Mark Thomas

Mark Thomas's grandfather (Mal Thomas's father-in-law) was the Warrington forward Ivor Bennett. Dave Cotton snr's younger son, Fran, was the multi-capped England rugby union prop forward. Alex Murphy's father James had trials with Warrington's 'A' team in the 1920s. A third generation Keith Holden, an England under-16 hooker, is learning his trade with the Warrington academy squads.

MADE IN WALES

In the early days of the club, all the players came from Warrington. As the club's fame spread, however, players were recruited from further afield. The first Welshman to play for the Wirepullers came from South Wales and his surname was Bowen – no doubt he was recommended to the committee by an agent. Bowen was said to be so fast 'he could catch pigeons'. The Warrington-based players were told this and stepped up their training so that they would be able to keep up with this Welsh superman. Bowen arrived in the town on the Saturday morning and was immediately handed his debut. What a disappointment! Bowen turned out to be more pigeon-toed than pigeon-catcher. Warrington lost the match and Bowen was never seen again.

CAPTAIN MORGAN TROPHY

The Captain Morgan Trophy was only played for once, in the 1973/74 season, and Warrington won it. From day one, it was a bit of an oddity in an already crowded fixture list. To qualify you had to win your County Cup first-round tie, which Warrington did by beating Leigh. Victories over Wigan, Castleford and Leeds followed before Warrington beat Featherstone Rovers 4–0 in the final at The Willows thanks to two 45-yard penalty goals from man of the match Derek Whitehead.

Warrington: Whitehead; M. Philbin, Noonan, Reynolds, Bevan; Whittle, Gordon; Chisnall, Ashcroft, Brady, Wanbon, D. Wright, Mather. Subs: Pickup, Price.

PRIMROSE AND BLUE

Warrington are famous for playing in primrose and blue, but they were not the club's first colours. The first mention of the club's colours dates from the annual general meeting of September 1879, held at the Patten Arms pub, when they wore narrow scarlet and black hoops. The switch to primrose and blue came in December 1886 for the visit of Wigan when Warrington wore narrow primrose and blue stripes with turned-down collars. It is thought that Warrington switched colours to impress the wealthy Greenall family, owners of the Greenall Whitley brewery, who lived at Walton Hall. The Greenalls were keen supporters of the Primrose League and, of course, true blue Tories. The Primrose League was founded in 1883 with the aim of spreading Conservative values in Great Britain and by 1886 it may have had as many as one million members. Another theory is that Lady Daresbury was asked to choose the new colours and picked primrose because it was her favourite flower.

Warrington released a single called 'Primrose and blue' during the all-conquering 1973/74 season. Available on the Liverpool Sound (Enterprises) Limited label, it featured vocals by the Wire Choir – the Warrington RL team and supporters – and music from an electronic organ. The song began 'Primrose and blue, for me and for you, they're the colours we all love to see' and continued in a similar vein. For some reason, it was not able to dislodge 'Waterloo' by Abba from the number one slot.

Warrington-born Steve Donoghue was the most famous jockey in the land in the 1920s – and a keen supporter of the Wire. He won the Derby six times – in 1915, 1917, 1921, 1922, 1923 and 1925 – and was Champion Jockey on ten occasions. When his days as a jockey were over, he became a trainer and registered his own racing colours – primrose and blue hoops – in tribute to the Wire.

Another Warrington-born Champion Jockey, Paul Hanagan, who was the Champion Jockey in 2010 and 2011, is a patron of the Warrington Wolves Foundation, the club's registered charity. He made a guest appearance at the Warrington versus Leeds match in March 2011 and was presented with his official patronage certificate by Councillor Terry O'Neill, the chairman of the foundation.

BOOTS AND ALL

Legend has it that Warrington's first player from New Zealand, the Maori Dick Papakura, played in bare feet when he made his only appearance for the club against Broughton

Rangers at Wilderspool in October 1911. It's probably not true but it's a good story. Second-row forward Mark Roberts missed the 1989 Lancashire Cup semi-final against Widnes, the newly crowned World Club Champions, at Wilderspool through injury. Centre Tony Thorniley borrowed his boots and scored 2 tries as Warrington recorded a famous 28–6 victory. New Zealand forward Louis Anderson gave his boots away to some supporters in the joyous scenes after Warrington won the Challenge Cup at Wembley in 2009.

STRIKE ACTION

Warrington's first team have been on strike twice, both times over money and both times the industrial action quickly fizzled out. The first strike was in September 1895, three games into the Northern Union era. Some of the players had claimed 9s each in expenses, for broken time and tea money, for the game at Bradford which Warrington had lost 23–0. The Warrington committee, however, insisted that no broken time had taken place because the players had not left Warrington until 12.55 p.m. and so could still have gone to work on the Saturday morning.

The second strike was in January 1914 over the non-payment of a £1 per man winning bonus – which is roughly £500 per man at today's prices. Again, the dispute ended quickly but the governing body, the Northern Union, still decided not to consider any Warrington players for that summer's tour of Australia and New Zealand because of their 'acts of insubordination'. Full-back Ben Jolley and forwards John Willie Chesters, Percy Clare and Harry Cox all had strong claims to be included and were even nominated by the club. None of the four would ever tour, with Jolley being particularly unlucky. He suffered a broken leg at home to Dewsbury in January 1920, ruling him out of that summer's trip to Australia and New Zealand as well.

ROLL OF HONOUR

More than 90 Warrington players and past players (including reserve team players) served their king and country during the First World War. Tragically, 11 of them perished in the conflict. The full roll of honour is as follows:

Sergeant Howard Davis, of the Rifle Brigade, who died aged 27, on 31 July 1915. He had made 22 appearances for the first team between 1912 and 1915, scoring 1 try.

Private James Andrews, of the South Lancashire Regiment, who died on 10 August 1915. He had made 49 appearances for the first team between 1895 and 1900.

Rifleman James Berry, of the Rifle Brigade, who died aged 48, on 8 September 1915. He had played for the first team for about 5 years, mainly in the club's rugby union days.

Rifleman Joseph Oakes, of the Rifle Brigade, who died aged 31 on 25 September 1915. He was a former 'A' team player who had also played for the Runcorn and Cadishead clubs.

Private George Thomas, of the South Lancashire Regiment, who died aged 35, on Monday 3 July 1916. He had made 385 first team appearances, scoring 47 tries and kicking 198 goals.

Private John Stuntz, of the Australian Infantry, who died on Thursday 3 May 1917. He had scored 13 tries in 19 appearances during the 1909/10 season.

Private Stanley Young, of the Manchester Regiment, who died aged 29 on 18 April 1918. He had made 60 appearances from 1913 to 1915, scoring 2 tries.

Private John Cartwright, of the Welsh Guards, who died aged 34 on 3 May 1918, leaving a wife and five children. He had made 33 appearances for the first team from 1906 to 1910, scoring 5 tries.

Three more 'A' team players – Alec Brown, Dalby Newall and E.J. Burton – also perished, although less is known about exactly when and where they met their deaths.

A Warrington player also lost his life during the Second World War. Flying officer Frank Cueto, aged 27, a member of the Royal Air Force Volunteer Reserve, died on 9 February 1944 when his fighter plane went down in the English Channel. He had made 79 appearances from 1936 to 1940, scoring 10 tries, and was a member of the 1937 Lancashire Cup winning side. He had already represented his native Cumberland and had been tipped as a future Great Britain scrum-half.

TRY AND TRY AGAIN

On two occasions Brian Bevan scored tries in a club record 11 consecutive matches. His first glory run was from 28 August to 11 October 1948 during which he crossed for 23 tries. He repeated the feat from 25 August to 30 October 1954, again scoring 23 tries. Bob Eccles holds the record for a Warrington forward after scoring tries in 9 consecutive matches from 26 September to 14 November 1982 – he scored 1 try in each game. Four players have scored tries in 7 consecutive Super League games: Nigel Vagana (1997), Toa Kohe-Love (1999), Chris Hicks (2008) and Richie Myler (2011).

NUMBERS GAME

Warrington wore numbers on their jerseys for the first time for a Lancashire Cup tie against Leigh at Wilderspool on

Saturday 28 October 1905. Rugby league was still a 15-a-side sport and so Warrington were numbered 1 to 15, but they still lost the match 5–2. Warrington wore squad numbers for the first time for round two of Super League I, against Workington Town at Wilderspool in April 1996, and won 45–30. The highest squad number issued by the club so far is the number 46 worn by David 'Doc' Murray when he made 3 substitute appearances at the end of Super League II – in August and September 1997.

NICKNAMES

Just about every player has a nickname, but here are some of the more unusual ones.

Mike 'Streaky' Bacon – was a winger
James 'Smack' Bate – clapped his hands once when he
    wanted the ball
Joe 'Surefoot' Boscow – never put a foot wrong
Brian 'Bully' Brady – because of his strength
Derek 'Nobby' Clarke
Billy 'Billy Whizz' Cowell
Jonathan 'Jiffy' Davies – because of his speed
Ronnie 'Rhino' Duane – because of his power
Don 'Mad Dog' Duffy – you had to see him in training
Arthur 'Candy' Evans
Chris 'Spider' Hicks
Mark 'The Beast' Hilton – because of his controlled
    aggression
Andrew 'Joey' Johns
Bill 'Massa' Johnston
Les 'Cowboy' Jones – had bandy legs
Allan 'Alfie' Langer
Gary 'Ming' Mercer – because of Ming the Merciless in
    Flash Gordon

Jack 'Cod' Miller – sold fish

Adrian 'Moz' Morley

Ces 'The Blackball Bullet' Mountford

David 'Doc' Murray

Harold 'Moggy' Palin – because of his cat-like agility

Alan 'Rambo' Rathbone – nobody's arguing

Bill 'Spiv' Riley – used to buy and sell goods

Steve 'Blocker' Roach – was an enforcer

Gary 'The Hoover' Sanderson – cleaned up lost possession

Paul 'Scully' Sculthorpe – Sculthorpe is too long

Kevin 'Terrible' Tamati – as in Ivan the Terrible, the Russian
    Tsar, as in absolutely terrifying

George 'Ponty' Thomas – played for Pontnewydd

Tommy 'Tubby' Thompson – because of his midriff

James 'Tosh' Thorniley

Tony 'Too Tall' Thorniley – after wearing a neck brace

Robert 'Rocky' Turner – it goes with the surname

Brendon 'the baby-faced assassin' Tuuta

Lee Briers tried to call himself 'The Axe' after chopping someone down with a crunching tackle, but it never caught on. Sorry Lee. 'Moggy' Palin did not like his nickname, which he was given as a teenager, but it stuck.

PLAYER OF THE 1900S – JACK FISH (1898–1911)

Jack Fish was Warrington's first superstar and singlehandedly rewrote the club's record books. He was a brilliant winger with pace to burn, an incredible swerve and the ability to stop dead in his tracks and then regain top speed again almost immediately. This latter trick often left opponents whizzing into touch. He was also the star attraction in Warrington's first great three-quarter line – Jack Fish, Danny Isherwood, George Dickenson, Elliot Harris – who were christened the 'Aristocratic Four' and who tormented opposition defences for the best part of 5 years. Remarkably, on two occasions in 1900, the first letters of the surnames of the three-quarter line actually spelt out FISH; first when it was Fish, Isherwood, Llandaff Smith and Harris and three weeks later when it was Fish, Isherwood, Smith and Tom Hockenhull.

Fish was the first Warrington player to score a hat-trick of tries and the first to score 5 tries in a match, 20 tries in a season and 100 tries in a career. He also played for Lancashire and scored England's first try in rugby league's first international match. When Warrington won the Challenge Cup for the first time in 1905, he scored both their tries. Two years later, he was the captain when Warrington won the cup for the second time. This time he scored a spectacular, long-range try and kicked 4 goals. He also scored tries against Australia and New Zealand. The fans loved him and wore metal, fish-shaped badges at big matches to show their support. For the 1904 Challenge Cup final, however, one group of Warrington fans decided that metal badges of fish were not enough. They wanted the real thing and went to Warrington Fish Market on the morning of the match to buy it. At the final, every time Fish got the ball, they tossed pieces of fish into the air which then dropped on to other supporters. Fish later spent one season as Warrington coach, 1927/28, and guided the team to yet another final.

When he died, aged 61, in October 1940, supporters lined the streets as the funeral cortège made its way to Warrington Cemetery to pay their silent tribute to a great entertainer. Fish was, without doubt, a larger-than-life character and perhaps that explains why, according to a local newspaper article from the 1980s, his ghost still haunts the Arpley area of the town.

Appearances: 321
Tries: 214
Goals: 263
Points: 1,168

Honours: Challenge Cup 1904/05 and 1906/07.

DROP GOAL KINGS

The club's all-time leading drop goal kickers are as follows:

1	Lee Briers	68
2	Steve Hesford	47
3	Paul Bishop	42
4	Willie Aspinall	30
5	Alex Murphy	28
6	Jonathan Davies	26
7	Kevin Ashcroft	23
8	Derek Whitehead	21
9	Greg Mackey	20

From the birth of rugby league in 1895 until the summer of 1974, drop goals were worth 2 points each. From the start of the 1974/75 season they were decreased in value to 1 point. Alex Murphy kicked Warrington's last 2-point drop goal in the Challenge Cup final victory over Featherstone Rovers at Wembley. Kevin Ashcroft kicked the first 1-pointer against Widnes at Wilderspool that August, although having been in Australia with Great Britain all summer he thought they were still worth 2 points.

Lee Briers and Paul Bishop have both kicked a club record 5 drop goals in a match. Bishop drop kicked his 5 against Wigan in a Premiership Trophy semi-final at Central Park in May 1986 as Warrington scored a famous 23–12 victory. Briers bagged his quintet in a Super League match at Halifax in May 2002, but Warrington still lost 16–11.

Briers kicked arguably the most important drop goal in the club's history in the Challenge Cup quarter-final at Hull Kingston Rovers in May 2009 to seal a thrilling 25–24 victory in golden point extra time. Warrington went on to win the cup.

Warrington were on the receiving end of the longest drop goal in RL history when Wigan centre Joe Lydon landed a monster 1-pointer in the Challenge Cup semi-final at Maine Road in March 1989. Lydon's kick was from inside his own half and was officially measured after the match as being from 61 yards (55 metres). It came in the 73rd minute and edged Wigan ahead 7–6 and on their way to a 13–6 victory. To this day, Warrington fans maintain that it was a fluke.

RECORD CROWDS

The record crowd for a match at Wilderspool was the 34,304 who attended the league game between Warrington and Wigan on 22 January 1949. Warrington lost 8–4. All 35,000 tickets for the 1949 Lancashire Cup final between Wigan and Leigh at Wilderspool 9 months later were sold, but only 33,701 actually attended.

The record crowd for a match at The Halliwell Jones Stadium was the 14,206 who attended the opening game against Wakefield in the Super League on Saturday 21 February 2004. Supporters who arrived late found the turnstiles locked because of congestion on the terraces. A rumour started that 2,000 fans had been locked out, although the actual figure was about 250 and they were admitted 20 minutes into the match.

The delay meant that they missed the first try at the new stadium, scored by scrum-half Nathan Wood and converted by captain Lee Briers. After those rather chaotic scenes, the capacity of the ground was reduced slightly to 13,024. However, in March 2011 Warrington announced plans for a £2 million extension to the ground that will take the capacity up to 15,500, making a new record crowd possible and, indeed, likely. Warrington's last 15,000 home crowd was in March 1973 when 15,600 saw the Wire lose to Featherstone 18–14 in the third round of the Challenge Cup.

CROWD PLEASERS

Warrington have played in front of some huge crowds. Here are the top 10:

1   102,569 for Warrington 8–4 Halifax (1954 Challenge Cup replay, Odsal)

2   94,249 for Warrington 19–0 Widnes (1950 Challenge Cup final, Wembley)

3   85,217 for Warrington 30–6 Leeds (2010 Challenge Cup final, Wembley)

4   85,098 for Widnes 14–7 Warrington (1975 Challenge Cup final, Wembley)

5   81,841 for Warrington 4–4 Halifax (1954 Challenge Cup final, Wembley)

6   77,729 for Wigan 36–14 Warrington (1990 Challenge Cup final, Wembley)

7   77,400 for Warrington 24–9 Featherstone (1974 Challenge Cup final, Wembley)

8   76,560 for Warrington 25–16 Huddersfield (2009 Challenge Cup final, Wembley)

9   75,194 for Huddersfield 13–12 Warrington (1949 Championship final, Maine Road)

10   69,898 for Warrington 16–4 Leeds (1950 Challenge Cup semi-final, Odsal)

The 102,569 crowd for the 1954 Challenge Cup final replay remained a world record attendance for an RL game for 45 years until 107,999 attended the 1999 NRL Grand Final between Melbourne Storm and St George Illawarra Dragons at the Telstra Stadium, the former Olympic Stadium, in Sydney. Future Warrington forwards Paul Marquet and Tawera Nikau played for Melbourne, who won a thrilling match 20–18. Future Warrington prop Chris Leikvoll was in the losing St George side. The 1954 Challenge Cup final replay inspired a book *There Were a Lot More Than That* which argues convincingly that although 102,569 was the official attendance the actual crowd was closer to 120,000. The 69,898 crowd who watched Warrington beat Leeds at Odsal in 1950 remains a record attendance for a Challenge Cup semi-final.

TAKING AN EARLY BATH

Welsh forward Mike Nicholas was Warrington's cleanest player, but only because he was asked to take an early bath 13 times during his remarkable 8-year career. His cleanest (or dirtiest) season was 1978/79 when he got first use of the hot water on four occasions.

At one time, getting sent off was almost an occupational hazard for a Warrington forward, although the club's backs have also incurred the referee's displeasure. Even the club's greatest player, the Australian winger Brian Bevan, was sent off once, at Widnes on Christmas Day 1948, for a 'stiff-arm tackle' on winger Stan Jolley. Bevan's challenge was more clumsy than malicious but still earned him a 2-match ban.

IN THE BIN

The sin bin was introduced on 1 January 1983 and the first Warrington player to pay it a visit was prop Dave Chisnall in the league game at Barrow on 16 January for a high tackle on Ron O'Regan. Chissie had only come on as a half-time substitute for Tony Cooke. Australian prop Andrew Gee must have liked the sin bin: he was sent there six times during the 2000 season. Another Australian forward, Bob Jackson, was the first Warrington player to visit the blood bin – after 10 minutes of the home game against Salford at Wilderspool on 1 September 1991. Don Duffy took Jackson's place for 6 minutes while he was patched up. Welsh forward Mark Jones was the first Warrington player to be put on report, at Bradford in August 1995. When the RFL's disciplinary committee reviewed the incident they hit him with a 2-match ban.

NEW TECHNOLOGY

The league match between Warrington and Halifax at Wilderspool on 2 January 1932 was the first to be broadcast on radio – Warrington lost 2–0. Hospital radio made its Wilderspool debut in February 1953 for the Challenge Cup tie against Workington Town, the holders. George Duckworth, the Warrington-born former Lancashire and England wicket-keeper, led the commentary team as the Wire won 10–2. Duckworth's uncle, Jack Duckworth, had played for Warrington in the 1901 Challenge Cup final against Batley at Headingley.

Satellite television, in the shape of Sky Sports and their commentators Eddie Hemmings and the former Great Britain international hooker Mike 'Stevo' Stephenson, made its first visit to Wilderspool in October 1992. Bradford Northern were the visitors and they won 22–4 with Warrington's try coming from winger Neil Kenyon.

The video referee made his first appearance at Wilderspool for the Super League game against Halifax on Friday 12 April 1996. He denied Warrington a try, but awarded one to Halifax centre Asa Amone.

Warrington's Super League game at Wigan in July 2010 was the first to be shown by Sky in 3D – Warrington won 23–16. The 2010 Challenge Cup final between Warrington Wolves and Leeds Rhinos at Wembley was the first to be shown in high definition.

HIGH FIVES

Winger Jack Fish was the first Warrington player to score at least 5 tries in a match, against Goole at Wilderspool in the second round of the Challenge Cup in March 1900. Here is the full list of players who have achieved the feat:

7	Brian Bevan v Leigh	H	29 March 1948	Lge
7	Brian Bevan v Bramley	H	22 April 1953	Lge
6	Tommy Thompson v Bradford	H	6 April 1933	Lge
6	Brian Bevan v York	H	23 Sep 1950	Lge
6	Brian Bevan v Rochdale	H	17 Nov 1951	Lge
6	Brian Bevan v Bramley	A	17 Feb 1954	Chall Cup
6	Brian Bevan v Liverpool	H	13 Nov 1954	Lge
5	Jack Fish v Goole	H	24 March 1900	Chall Cup
5	Bert Bradshaw v St Helens	H	12 April 1909	Lge
5	George Thomas v St Helens	H	12 April 1909	Lge
5	Steve Ray v Wigan Highfield	H	4 March 1933	Lge
5	Islwyn 'Izzy' Davies v Leigh	H	17 April 1939	Lge
5	Brian Bevan v Oldham	H	17 April 1948	Lge
5	Brian Bevan v Oldham	H	28 Sept 1948	Lancs Cup
5	Brian Bevan v Oldham	A	2 Oct 1948	Lge
5	Brian Bevan v Liverpool	A	8 Nov 1952	Lge
5	Brian Bevan v Orford Tannery	H	7 Feb 1953	Chall Cup
5	Albert Naughton v Belle Vue	A	5 March 1955	Lge
5	Brian Bevan v Rochdale	H	30 April 1958	Lge
5	Terry O'Grady v Featherstone	H	9 Sept 1961	Lge

5	Parry Gordon v Dewsbury	H	3 March 1974	Lge
5	Bob Eccles v Blackpool	H	12 Dec 1982	John Player
5	Chris Riley v Harlequins	H	7 Feb 2010	Super League
5	Chris Bridge v Huddersfield	A	8 May 2010	Chall Cup

Chris Riley's 5 tries against Harlequins is the club's Super League record.

PLAYER OF THE 1910s – GEORGE THOMAS (1903–14)

Welsh forward George Thomas was another Warrington player who made an indelible mark on the club's record books. When Warrington thrashed St Helens 78–6 on Easter Monday 1909, Thomas helped himself to 5 tries and kicked 8 goals for a match haul of 31 points and a record that stood for 90 years. Thomas had signed for the Wirepullers from Newport in August 1903 but had learned his rugby skills at the Pontnewydd club, hence his nickname Ponty. When he first arrived at Wilderspool, some members of the committee questioned his small stature for a forward: he was only 5ft 8in and 12st. Thomas replied by stating that, 'Good stuff lies in little room.' So it proved, although there were some suggestions that he might have been better off operating at stand-off, but that would never have suited his all-action, tough-tackling style.

He played in four Challenge Cup finals for Warrington, collecting winners' medals in 1905 and 1907 and finishing on the losing side in 1904 and 1913. Thomas was also outspoken, and that almost certainly cost him a place on the first Great Britain tour to Australia and New Zealand in 1910. When Warrington's first-team players went on strike in January 1914, for example, over the non-payment of a £1 bonus, it was Thomas who addressed the 4,000-strong Wilderspool crowd after an 'A' team game to explain their differences. Thomas did, however, play for Wales against the New Zealand All Golds in January 1908. Following the outbreak of the First World War in August 1914, he was one of the first to enlist and joined the South Lancashire regiment. He continued to keep himself fit and won the 5-mile race for his company. In April 1916, Thomas, who was a private, sent a letter home from the Western Front. Showing extreme candour and courage, he wrote, 'I have had some trying times on the football field and our side usually came out on top but as true as there is a drop of British blood runs through my veins I hope to give the Germans a sound thrashing. But if I should fall you can tell the boys I fell fighting like a hero should do for his King and country.'

In late June 1916, Thomas was made a colonel's orderly before, in the early hours of Monday 3 July 1916, he was killed in action on the Somme, aged 35. An eyewitness reported that he was 'blown to pieces' by a German shell.

Appearances: 385
Tries: 47
Goals: 198
Points: 537

Honours: Challenge Cup 1904/05 and 1906/07.

MAN OF STEEL

Only two Warrington players have been crowned Man of Steel since the award was introduced in 1977. The Man of Steel, or player of the season, is the highest individual honour in the British game. Warrington's winners were:

Ken Kelly, 1980/81. The Warrington scrum-half and captain led the side to a Lancashire Cup and John Player Trophy double and to the semi-finals of the Challenge

Cup. Warrington also finished second in the Slalom Lager Championship. Kelly was also named First Division player of the year.

Jonathan Davies, 1993/94. Like Ken Kelly, Warrington's Welsh centre was also named First Division player of the year after an outstanding season. 'Jiffy' was Warrington's leading try-scorer and goal-kicker and formed a world-class centre pairing with his fellow countryman Allan Bateman as the Wire missed out on the title only on points difference. Davies also worked his magic for Wales and Great Britain.

TOP TENS

The following Warrington players have kicked 10 goals or more in a match:

16	Lee Briers v Swinton	H	20 May 2011	Chall Cup
14	Lee Briers v York	H	27 Feb 2000	Chall Cup
14	Harold Palin v Liverpool Stanley	H	13 Sept 1950	Lancs Cup
13	Brett Hodgson v Harlequins	H	20 March 2011	SL
12	Harold Palin v York	H	23 Sept 1950	Lge
12	Lee Briers v Keighley	H	8 May 2011	Chall Cup
11	Ken Hindley v Barrow	H	8 Oct 1972	Lge
10	Harry Bath v Belle Vue	A	13 Sept 1952	Lge
10	Harry Bath v Bramley	H	22 April 1953	Lge
10	Harry Bath v Bramley	H	16 Jan 1954	Lge
10	Laurie Gilfedder v Liverpool City	H	31 Aug 1957	Lancs Cup
10	Derek Whitehead v Blackpool	H	11 March 1970	Lge
10	John Woods v Swinton	H	30 Sept 1987	Lancs Cup

10	Jonathan Davies v Workington	H	16 Oct 1994	Lge
10	Graham Appo v Wakefield	H	21 Sept 2003	SL
10	Lee Briers v Castleford	A	17 April 2006	SL
10	Brett Hodgson v Crusaders	H	15 April 2011	SL
10	Brett Hodgson v Salford	A	22 April 2011	SL
10	Chris Bridge v Wakefield	H	14 Aug 2011	SL

Graham Appo kicked his 10 goals from 10 attempts during the last Super League match at Wilderspool. In contrast, Warrington's worst goal-kicking performance came against Liverpool at Wilderspool in February 1907. Warrington scored 16 tries but could only convert 2 of them on their way to a 52–0 victory. Tom Hockenhull and Jack Preston kicked a goal apiece.

BLASTS FROM THE PAST

Warrington had to cancel or postpone a number of games in November and December 1892 because a smallpox epidemic was raging in the town. In December 1897, Warrington were ordered to put up 200 notices because of unruly conduct by spectators.

Days after making his Warrington debut against Salford in January 1900, forward Walter Ashton went to South Africa with the Warrington Volunteers to fight in the Boer War. Another Warrington forward, Arthur Naylor, also fought in the conflict with the Grenadier Guards. Naylor also fought throughout the First World War until he was shot by a sniper in 1917. The bullet passed through his ear, neck and back; 'But I am glad to tell you,' he wrote in a letter home, 'that I am improving. The doctors say that I am a very lucky man to be living.'

In April 1907, Warrington sent Widnes the sum of £20, equivalent to about £2,000 in today's money, to help ease their financial worries.

The first Wardonia Cup game, a pre-season friendly between Warrington and Wigan, was held at Central Park in August 1938. It ended 17–17 before Jack Arkwright, the Warrington captain, won the cup on the toss of a coin.

The late Ossie Peake is the only Warrington player – so far – to have scored 4 tries in a match against Wigan. Peake scored 2 in each half when Warrington thrashed the cherry and whites 36–8 at Wilderspool in September 1938.

AGE IS ONLY A NUMBER

Age is only a number but, sometimes, it can be a very big number. The oldest player to play for Warrington was second-row Jack Arkwright who achieved the feat at Hunslet in September 1945, aged 42 years and 9 months. Warrington's oldest try-scorer was hooker Dave Cotton who touched down against Huddersfield at Wilderspool in April 1948, aged 39.

Since the dawn of Super League, Warrington's oldest player is New Zealand prop Paul Rauhihi, who made his last appearance against Harlequins at The Halliwell Jones Stadium in September 2009, aged 36 years and 2 months. He was born on 3 July 1973. Winger Mark Forster is Warrington's oldest try-scorer of the Super League era, after touching down at Wakefield in September 2000, aged 35 years and 9 months.

The youngest player to play for Warrington was stand-off Jackie Edwards who made his debut against Wakefield Trinity at QPR's Loftus Road ground in an ITV Trophy match in November 1955, aged 16 years and 3 months. But Warrington's youngest try-scorer was centre Laurie Gilfedder who touched down at Halifax in March 1952, aged 16 years and 10 months.

In the Super League era, Warrington's youngest player is scrum-half John Duffy who made his debut against London Broncos at Wilderspool in March 1997, aged 16 years and

262 days. He was born on 2 July 1980. Their youngest try-scorer in the Super League era is winger Chris Riley, who scored as a substitute at Widnes in August 2005 – aged 17 years and 6 months. He was born on 22 February 1988. Warrington won that match 60–16 to relegate Widnes from Super League.

When winger Mike Kelly signed for Warrington in 1977 he said that he was 22, rather than 25, because he was worried that coach Alex Murphy would not want to sign a 25-year-old. The deception only came to light after Kelly died aged 56 – actually aged 59 – in 2011.

GLOBE TROTTERS

Warrington have played in 10 different countries as follows:

England (obviously)

Wales (including the Millennium Stadium)

Scotland (at Murrayfield in 2009 and 2010)

Northern Ireland (v Halifax at Windsor Park, Belfast, on Thursday 27 May 1954)

Republic of Ireland (v Wigan at Shelbourne Park, Dublin, on 12 May 1934 for the Irish Hospitals Trust Cup and v Halifax at Dalymount Park, Dublin, on Friday 28 May 1954 for the Dublin Copper Kettle)

United States of America (v Wigan at Milwaukee County Stadium on 10 June 1989 in the American Challenge match)

France (most recently at Perpignan)

Spain (v Catalans Dragons at the Olympic Stadium, Barcelona on 20 June 2009)

Australia (at Penrith Panthers and Cronulla Sharks in July 1997 as part of the World Club Challenge)

New Zealand (at Auckland Warriors in August 1997, also as part of the World Club Challenge)

Lee Briers is the club's most travelled player, having played in six different countries for Warrington: England, Wales, Scotland, France, Australia and New Zealand. It would have been seven but he missed the trip to Barcelona through injury. Warrington players have been to even more exotic climes while on tour with Great Britain. Laurie Gilfedder and Eric Fraser, for example, played in South Africa in 1962 while Mike Gregory played in Papua New Guinea in 1988 and twice in 1990. Iestyn Harris and Paul Sculthorpe played in Papua New Guinea and Fiji in 1996.

LANCE TODD TROPHY

Four Warrington players have won the Lance Todd Trophy for being the man of the match in the Challenge Cup final. Scrum-half Gerry Helme collected it in 1950 and 1954, becoming the first player to win it twice. He received it in 1950 after a commanding performance in the 19–0 victory over Widnes at Wembley. Four years later he was chosen again after scoring Warrington's second try in the 8–4 victory over Halifax in the Challenge Cup final replay at Odsal. After that it was decided that the Lance Todd Trophy would go to the man of the match at Wembley, even if the final ended in a draw and required a replay.

Full-back Derek Whitehead won the Lance Todd Trophy in 1974 after kicking 7 goals, from all angles and distances, in the 24–9 victory over Featherstone Rovers. Australian hooker Michael Monaghan became the first Warrington player to win the award at the new Wembley Stadium after scoring one of the four Wolves try in the 25–16 win over the Huddersfield Giants in 2009. Stand-off Lee Briers won the award 12 months later after an almost perfect display against Leeds Rhinos as the Wolves won 30–6.

POINTS MAKE PRIZES – PART I

Nine players have scored 1,000 points for the club:

1	Lee Briers (1997–)	2,466
2	Steve Hesford (1975–86)	2,416
3	Brian Bevan (1945–62)	2,288
4	Harry Bath (1948–57)	1,894
5	Billy Holding (1928–40)	1,686
6	Derek Whitehead (1969–79)	1,516
7	Jack Fish (1898–1911)	1,168
8	Laurie Gilfedder (1951–63)	1,140
9	Eric Fraser (1951–64)	1,096

HARRY SUNDERLAND TROPHY

The Harry Sunderland Trophy is presented to the man of the match in the end-of-season Championship, Premiership or Grand Final and has been awarded to two Warrington players. Loose-forward Barry Philbin received it for an outstanding display in the 1974 Club Championship final against St Helens at Wigan's Central Park, which Warrington won 13–12. Australian prop Les Boyd won it 12 years later after scoring 2 tries in the Premiership final victory over Halifax at Elland Road in May 1986. Warrington romped home 38–10, scoring 7 tries.

PLAYER OF THE 1920s –
BILLY CUNLIFFE (1914–30)

Prop-forward Billy Cunliffe was not short of headwear because he won 11 Great Britain caps, 10 England caps and made 19 appearances for Lancashire and they gave out caps too. He was also the first Warrington player to make two tours of Australia and New Zealand, in 1920 and again in 1924. On the long voyage to Australia from Tilbury in 1924, all 26 members of the Great Britain touring party were weighed and Billy, who tipped the scales at 14st 8lb, was the heaviest. No wonder he was such an effective scrummager! Billy, who was 5ft 10in, was the type of forward who could play his game to suit the occasion and his opponents soon learned to appreciate this. He could be skilful, but he could also be rough, tough and ruthless.

Billy had joined Warrington from Pemberton Rovers in 1914. His younger brother, Tom, a second-row forward, followed him to Wilderspool a few months later and the pair became mainstays of the Warrington pack. Billy was a member of two Lancashire Cup winning sides (in 1921 and 1929) and played in the 1926 Championship Final and 1928 Challenge Cup final teams, both of which saw Warrington beaten. He made his 438th and final appearance for the Wire against Wigan at Wilderspool in September 1930. Warrington lost 10–4 and Billy lost his place in the team. Reluctantly, 3 months later, he was allowed to join Broughton Rangers because he wanted to continue playing the game he loved. Off the field, he ran a pub, the Black Bull Hotel at Lamberhead Green, Wigan.

Appearances: 438
Tries: 38
Goals: 6
Points: 126

Honours: Lancashire Cup 1921/22 and 1929/30.

NAME GAMES

Leading rugby union clubs would be mortified but only one Warrington player has had a double-barrelled surname, the New Zealand-born centre Toa Kohe-Love.

Twelve Warrington players have had surnames made up of just three letters: Harry Cox (1912–15), George Cox (1922–3), Bryn Day (1947), Derek Day (1955), Terry Day (1983), J. Fox (1940), James Kay (1907–9), Frank Lee (1945–7), Jason Lee (1994–5), Steve Ray (1932–3), Kevin Rea (1989–91) and, most recently, the Australian prop Andrew Gee (2000-01).

Another Australian prop, Chris Leikvoll, was known as Chris 'Lightbulb' by some supporters. His unusual surname came from his Norwegian grandfather but because of this he had a European Union passport and did not count as an overseas player.

Another Australian forward, Steve Georgallis, made 10 appearances during the 2001 season before his career was ended by a ruptured Achilles tendon at Halifax. His family was of Greek extraction and he later captained and coached the fledgling Greek national side.

Only one Warrington player has had a surname beginning with the letter 'Q' – the aptly-named centre Mike Quick. Mateaki Mafi's middle name is the rather impressive Fonnama'atonga.

GOOD FRIDAY, BAD FRIDAY

Arthur Skelhorn, the former Warrington, Lancashire, England and Great Britain forward, refused to play or even watch rugby league on Good Fridays because of his strong religious beliefs. He would have been horrified at the thought of the team playing regularly on Sundays, as happens today. Skelhorn worshipped at St James's Church on Wilderspool Causeway and when he was selected for the 1920 tour of Australia and New Zealand the news was included in the parish magazine as follows: 'Mr Skelhorn is a regular attendant at St James's and we take it as an additional honour to the Church.' Skelhorn's full name was George Arthur Skelhorn – GAS for short.

POINTS MAKE PRIZES – PART II

Only two Warrington players have scored more than 350 points for the club in a single season. The Australian forward Harry Bath racked up 363 points during the 1952/53 campaign, with his haul being made up of 13 tries and 162 goals in 40 appearances. He may have scored even more points, had he not been sent off twice that season. The Great Britain international John Woods accumulated 351 points in 1987/88. His total was made up of 13 tries, 147 goals and 5 drop goals from 37 appearances. The most points scored by the team in a single season was the 1,359 accumulated in 2011, at the rate of 42 points per game. This included a club record 1,072 in the regular Super League season.

SUPERSUBS

Question: Who was Warrington's first substitute?
Answer: Centre Joe Pickavance who replaced the injured stand-off Willie Aspinall after 21 minutes of the opening match of the 1964/65 season against Leeds at Headingley. From the start of that season, substitutes were allowed for injuries, but only up to half time. It was to be another 5 years before substitutes were allowed at any time for any reason.

Question: Who was Warrington's earliest substitute?
Answer: Australian forward Don Duffy who replaced centre Tony Thorniley after 5 minutes of the game against Runcorn in the first round of the Regal Trophy in December

1990. Thorniley had suffered a sprung shoulder during the warm-up and bravely started the match before bowing to the inevitable. He was, however, back in time to collect a winners' medal in the final.

Question: Who has made the most substitute appearances in a single season?
Answer: Samoan prop Danny Lima who entered the fray from the bench 28 times in 2005.

Question: Who was the first Warrington player to make 100 appearances off the bench?
Answer: Hooker Mark Gleeson, Martin's brother, who reached his century in 2008.

Question: Who has made the most sub appearances for Warrington?
Answer: Prop Paul Wood, who had left the bench 151 times by the end of the 2011 season.

Question: Will you please pick two supersubs?
Answer: Hooker Mickey Higham collected Challenge Cup winners' medals at Wembley in 2009 and 2010 from the interchange bench. That will take some beating. And for older readers there is an honourable mention for forward Mark Thomas. The Wire were losing 6–0 to Second Division Oldham in the 1990 Challenge Cup semi-final at Central Park when coach Brian Johnson told him to join the action. Thomas quickly produced two inspired passes to create tries for scrum-half Martin Crompton and winger Mark Forster and Warrington were going to Wembley. Thomas repeated the feat in the 1991 Regal Trophy final against Bradford Northern at Headingley when he again entered the fray from the bench and scored the only try as Warrington won 12–2.

SUPERFAN

Postman Craig Garner has not missed a Warrington match since Bradford away on 3 March 1985 when, against his better judgment, he took a young lady to a basketball game. Since then he has not missed a match, home or away, clocking up more than 800 consecutive appearances in the process. If he were a player he would be in the club's Hall of Fame by now. His 26-year odyssey has taken him to Australia, New Zealand, the United States, France, Spain, Scotland and Wales. It must be in the blood because his great-great-grandfather was James Edward Warren, Ted Warren to his friends, the former Wire half-back, captain and secretary from the 1880s and 1890s. Indeed, it was Warren who represented the club at the George Hotel, Huddersfield on Thursday 29 August 1895 when the 21 northern clubs decided to break away from the Rugby Football Union and form the Northern Union. The rest, as they say, is history.

SEVENS UP

Warrington won the Wigan Sevens for the first and only time and so collected the Silcock Cup at Central Park on Saturday 7 August 1965. Warrington beat Widnes 19–15 in a thrilling final – a score made more dramatic by a stirring Widnes rally after Warrington had built up a 19–5 lead. A 75-yard try from Brian Glover had put Warrington ahead right from the kick-off. Warrington's magnificent seven were Martin Dickens, Billy Hayes, Parry Gordon, Peter Ashcroft, Geoff Robinson, Bobby Greenough and Brian Glover. Ray Fisher took over from Glover, who picked up a slight leg strain for the final.

SHIRT SPONSORS

Shirt sponsorship was introduced before the start of the 1983/84 season and has been a valuable source of funds ever since. Warrington's shirt sponsors have been:

Sparkomatic (1983–6)	3 seasons
Vladivar (1986–9)	3 seasons
Greenalls (1989–99)	11 seasons
Tetley's (2000–1)	2 seasons
Miller (2002–3)	2 seasons
Omega (2004–8)	5 seasons
Vestas (2009–10)	2 seasons
Bensons for Beds (2011–12)	2 seasons

In 1999, the home shirt had 'Greenalls' on the front while the away shirt had 'John Smith'. Greenalls had been bought out but it was too late to change the logo on the home shirt.

FIVE SENT OFF

It is not unusual for one or two players to be sent off in a match but FIVE is quite extraordinary. It happened in a Lancashire Cup second round tie at St Helens in September 1983. The Wire were leading 6–2 when tempers boiled over and Leigh referee Stan Wall sent off five players for fighting – Roy Haggerty and Steve Peters of St Helens plus Phil Ford, Mal Yates and Mark Forster of Warrington. Bob Eccles and Mike Gregory were also sent to the sin bin for 10 minutes each so that on two occasions Warrington were reduced to nine men. Yet, somehow, they still managed to win 30–6. Full-back Steve Hesford played his part with a try and 5 goals, John Bevan and Ronnie Duane were outstanding in the centres, Ken Kelly was magnificent at scrum-half, and the second-row partnership of Eccles and John Fieldhouse was immense. Inexplicably, Warrington then lost 19–18 at home to Second Division Barrow in the semi-finals.

FOUR SENT OFF

Four players were sent off – two from each side – in the annual pre-season 'friendly' against Wigan for the Locker Cup in August 1978. A Wigan official also doused a section of the crowd with a bucket of cold water. Hooker John Dalgreen and prop Roy Lester were sent off for Warrington, while Ron Dootson and John Wood walked for Wigan.

Four players were sent off and one sin binned during the Warrington versus Wigan derby on New Year's Day 1988. Warrington coach Tony Barrow later described it as 'World War Three'. The game exploded as early as the 9th minute when a brawl broke out after a clash between Les Boyd and Shaun Edwards. When it subsided, Wigan's Kiwi forward Adrian Shelford and Warrington's Tony Humphries were sent off. Referee Kevin Allatt also put Boyd in the sin bin.

Worse was to follow in the 20th minute after Wigan loose-forward Andy Goodway was sent off for a high tackle on Paul Cullen. As Goodway walked to the tunnel Cullen chased after him and launched himself at the Wigan player. A new brawl broke out and Cullen and Goodway had to be separated before the Warrington centre was also dismissed. Cullen's moment of madness probably cost Warrington victory in a game that ended in a 15–15 draw. It also earned him a two-match ban and ended his hopes of one day playing for Great Britain. 'I spoke with the then GB coach Mal Reilly immediately after that game and whatever international prospects I had at that time finished there and then,' Cullen later recalled.

PICK! PICK!

Warrington's Challenge Cup semi-final against Wakefield Trinity at Station Road, Swinton, in April 1963 turned on a moment that has now entered club folklore. Seven minutes from time, centre Joe Pickavance made a 40-yard break to the Wakefield '25' with half-backs Jackie Edwards and Bobby Greenough in support and Brian Glover coming up on the wing. Inexplicably, Pickavance kicked ahead and Wakefield – in the shape of Great Britain centre Neil Fox – gathered the ball to end the danger. Legend has it that Pickavance thought he heard Edwards shout 'Kick! Kick!' and so he kicked the ball when what the scrum-half had actually shouted was 'Pick! Pick!' because he wanted a pass. Warrington lost 5–2.

LIFESAVERS

Scrum-half Paul Bishop's second appearance for Warrington against Oldham at Wilderspool in November 1984 almost ended in tragedy. The 17-year-old was on the receiving end of a hard, but fair, tackle from winger Green Vigo and swallowed his tongue. Bishop started having convulsions but physiotherapist Gordon Pinkney, helped by coaches Derek Whitehead and Tony Barrow, managed to release the tongue and save his life.

KING COAL

Warrington won the second – and final – British Coal Nines tournament at Central Park on 2 November 1988 in front of 7,141 fans. BBC TV's *Sportsnight*'s cameras were there to see Warrington beat Wigan 12–6 in the first round, St Helens 6–0 in the semi-finals and the Rest of the World 24–0 in the final to pocket a £6,000 prize. John Woods was voted the man of the tournament as Mike Gregory captained a home-grown squad that also included Dave Lyon, Brian Carbert, John Thursfield, Mark Forster, Ronnie Duane, Billy McGinty, Mark Roberts, Gary Sanderson and Robert Turner. Warrington's three short-term Australian signings that season – Phil Blake, Les Davidson and Steve Roach – were allowed to miss the tournament and go sightseeing in Paris instead.

QUEEN'S HONOURS

Four Warrington players have been honoured by Her Majesty the Queen. Ces Mountford, the former Warrington player and coach, was made an MBE for services to sport in 1987 while Jonathan Davies was made an MBE in 1995 for services to both codes of rugby. Alex Murphy was awarded the OBE in 1998 for services to rugby league and, as usual, he was not lost for words, saying, 'It was a massive surprise when I got the letter from the Prime Minister. I thought it was a tax demand! It took me a few minutes to realise what it was! I was shell-shocked.' Throughout his playing career, Murphy had had many run-ins with the referee 'Sergeant Major' Eric Clay but insisted on taking the official to Buckingham Palace with him as one of his guests for the awards ceremony. Tommy Sale, then 92, was made an MBE in 2011.

Continuing the royal theme, when Widnes made their first visit to Wilderspool as a Super League club, on Easter Monday 2002, some of their supporters let the side down by chanting through a minute's silence to mourn the death of the Queen Mother. Off with their heads!

SILENT TRIBUTE

The town of Warrington hit the national headlines in tragic circumstances on Saturday 20 March 1993 when an IRA bomb exploded in the town centre, killing two young boys. A minute's silence was immaculately observed at Wilderspool before the St Helens game 8 days later and a ground collection in aid of the Warrington Bomb Appeal Support Fund raised a then record £1,945.

MURPHY THE MOUTH

More words of wisdom from Alexander the Great:

'It's going to be the survival of the fittest. You don't go to Wembley to entertain, you go to win the cup.'
Days before the 1974 Challenge Cup final at Wembley

'Things can go wrong. After all, the *Titanic* sank, didn't it?'
Minutes after the 1975 Challenge Cup final defeat to Widnes

'John Dorahy will come back to haunt Wigan – and that is a promise.'
Unveiling Dorahy as Warrington coach in January 1996

'Paul Newlove is the world's best centre and Toa Kohe-Love went past him as though he wasn't there. He made him look like a rocking horse.'
After 19-year-old Kohe-Love scored a superb try against St Helens in May 1996

MARATHON MEN

Well, actually, half-marathon men. Five Warrington players took part in the inaugural Warrington Half Marathon in October 2009, with captain Adrian Morley leading the way. Despite weighing 105kg (16st 7lbs) he was the first of the five to finish – a clear indication of his exceptional fitness levels. His time was a respectable 1 hour 47 minutes and 28 seconds and he finished ahead of Chris Riley (1hr 55.22), Lee Mitchell (1hr 57.44), Brian Carney (2hrs 7.18) and Paul Wood (2hrs 11.3).

PLAYER OF THE 1930s – BILLY DINGSDALE (1928–40)

Billy Dingsdale was Warrington's classiest centre and scored their first try at Wembley, against Huddersfield in the 1933 Challenge Cup final. It was one of 154 he scored in 373 appearances between 1928 and 1940 and he created dozens more for his winger Tommy 'Tubby' Thompson. He also perfected a skill that is rarely seen today; approaching an opponent at top speed, he would chip the ball over his head using the outside of his boot, accelerate round the player and catch it before it landed. Please don't try that at home.

Billy had signed for Warrington from Broughton Rangers in September 1928 for £600 – at a time when the world record fee was only £1,000. In his first season he quickly proved his worth by scoring 28 tries in 33 appearances to equal the club record set by Jack Fish. Billy was unlucky to play for Warrington at a time when they were the nearly men of rugby league, so although he played in two Challenge Cup finals (1933 and 1936) and two Championship Finals (1935 and 1937), the Wire lost the lot. He did, however, collect Lancashire Cup winners' medals in 1929 and 1932 and made 14 appearances for Lancashire, earning the accolade 'the doyen of Lancashire centres'. In 1932 he was selected for the Great Britain tour of Australia and New Zealand – the only Warrington player to make the trip – but what should have been the highlight of his career turned out to be a big disappointment because he could only play a handful of games owing to injury. When he retired from playing, he became the landlord of the Stanley Arms pub in St Helens for 25 years. He died in hospital in St Helens in 1965, aged 60.

Appearances: 373
Tries: 154
Goals: 4
Points: 470

Honours: Lancashire Cup 1929/30 and 1932/33
Lancashire League 1937/38.

STRANGE BUT TRUE

Warrington's league game at Oldham in the 1967/68 season was postponed six times: four times because of frost, once because Oldham were involved in a Challenge Cup replay and once because the Watersheddings pitch was waterlogged. Finally, on Monday 8 April 1968 – four months after it should have been played – the match went ahead and Warrington won 23–5.

Referee Fred Lindop failed to turn up for Warrington's home game against Hull KR on Friday 23 October 1970. He had received a hoax telephone call at his Wakefield home telling him that the stand had burned down and the match been postponed. Warrington referee Eric Lawrinson stepped in at the last minute. Twelve years later, on the lunchtime of Thursday 29 April 1982, the main stand did burn to the ground. Flames spread quickly across its whole length and within 20 minutes the largely timber frame was completely destroyed. The cause of the £300,000 blaze was never discovered, although it was thought that a cigarette discarded at the Warrington Amateur Cup final the previous evening could well have been responsible.

Warrington forward Geoff Clarkson missed the home game against Oldham in February 1972 in embarrassing circumstances. Instead of reporting to Wilderspool he went to the Watersheddings. His last-minute replacement in the Warrington team, Peter Cannon, crossed for the match-winning try in the last minute.

Warrington scrum-half Parry Gordon and St Helens stand-off Ken Kelly – later to be team-mates at Wilderspool – were sent off for fighting each other during the league match at Knowsley Road in August 1972.

Warrington coach Alex Murphy was not happy when the Wire were drawn at New Hunslet in the third round of the Challenge Cup in 1975. He objected to the American Football-style posts New Hunslet were using and which the Rugby Football League had, amazingly, approved. He said stripes should be painted on the in-goal area so that the players would not be confused. He said that if Hunslet did not do it he would send his own groundsman, Roy 'Ockher' Aspinall, to take care of the job. No matter, Warrington still won 23–3 cheered on by 4,000 travelling fans.

Warrington hooker Steve Moylan was left red-faced after forgetting to put his clock forward one hour to signal the start of British Summer Time on 31 March 1985. He arrived at Knowsley Road to find the game against St Helens had started, with Carl Webb wearing the number 9 shirt.

One of the ball boys at Wembley for the 1990 Challenge Cup final between Warrington and Wigan was a 12-year-old Oldham lad named Paul Sculthorpe. He signed for Warrington 4 years later.

Young winger Jason Lee played for Wales before he played for Warrington. Lee made his Wales debut as a substitute against Australia in Cardiff on 30 October 1994. He made his Wire debut, also against Australia, 10 days later.

Forward Shaun Geritas made only 8 appearances for Warrington. All were in 1997 and the Wolves lost every one.

Warrington's home game against Cronulla Sharks in June 1997 was interrupted by a male streaker.

Graham Appo was voted Warrington's 'coolest player' as part of a fans' poll by Tetley's on the Super League website in August 2003.

Warrington's Challenge Cup fourth round tie at Leigh in April 2008 proved to be too exciting for Arty, the home mascot. He was sent off by referee Steve Ganson for taking a touch judge's flag after Leigh had scored a try. Arty was led away by two stewards, wiping an imaginary tear away from his eyes.

FOUR GREAT COMEBACKS

17 December 1994, Salford 24–31 Warrington
At half time in this BBC-televised Regal Trophy tie at The Willows, Warrington were trailing 24–10 and seemed to be heading out of the competition before a storming second-half display turned the game on its head. Hooker Tukere Barlow scored the winning try after backing up a break by Bruce McGuire. Iestyn Harris added the goal and Kelly Shelford made the game safe with a drop goal.

28 May 2000, Warrington 42–32 Bradford
Warrington trailed the unbeaten Bulls by 18 points at half time (12–30) but, inspired by captain and scrum-half Allan Langer, who scored 2 tries, they pulled off an amazing victory. Centre Jon Roper also caught the eye with a try and 7 goals. The official club video described it as 'the best Super League game ever played at Wilderspool'.

26 March 2006, Wakefield 21–22 Warrington
Warrington trailed 21–0 after a dreadful first half but were transformed after the break to pull off what was then the

greatest comeback in Super League history. Young half-back Chris Bridge helped to save the day with 2 tries and 3 conversions.

26 July 2009, Warrington 62–20 Salford
Warrington trailed 20–12 at the interval before scoring 50 unanswered points in the second half. Salford coach Shaun McRae said, 'At half time, I was confident we would go on and win it but we went from grade A to Z.' Richie Myler scored a try for Salford but then Chris Bridge kicked 9 goals from 11 attempts and scored a try for Warrington.

FOUR GREAT ESCAPES

What, you may be asking, is the difference between a great comeback and a great escape? Hopefully, these four examples will explain everything.

15 February 1976, Warrington 16–12 Leigh Miners Welfare
Just two years after winning the Challenge Cup at Wembley, Warrington found themselves on the brink of one of the biggest shocks in the competition's history when the amateurs deservedly led 12–11 with time running out. Then Derek Whitehead, playing in the unaccustomed position of left centre, crossed for the match-winning try and added the conversion to seal a fortunate victory. Warrington were so impressed with one of the Miners forwards, John Whittaker, that they signed him.

15 November 1987, Carlisle 16–22 Warrington
Sitting in the Brunton Park press box before this John Player Trophy tie, the local reporter from Carlisle told me that you never saw shocks in rugby league. In the second half it looked like he was going to have to eat his words as Second Division Carlisle, coached by former Wire forward Roy

Lester, took control of the match to lead 16–8 with 16 minutes left. Thankfully for Warrington, stand-off John Woods then sold an outrageous dummy to score under the posts. He added the goal and levelled matters with a penalty before substitute Dave Lyon scored the winning try in the last minute. Woods had earlier scored the 3,000th point of his career with a 2nd-minute penalty goal. Carlisle forward Peter Subritzky was sent off 6 minutes from time for a high tackle that left Wire hooker Carl Webb with a broken jaw.

8 January 1995, Keighley Cougars 18–20 Warrington
With less than 15 minutes left in this Regal Trophy quarter-final, Warrington trailed 18–8 to Second Division Keighley and were on the brink of falling victim to Cougarmania. Winger Iestyn Harris then scored a try in the corner and full-back Jonathan Davies kicked a brilliant touchline conversion to throw Warrington a lifeline. Captain Greg Mackey denied Keighley winger Andy Eyres with a try-saving ankle tap before Davies weaved his way through a tiring defence to score. His conversion was cruel on Keighley but wonderful for Warrington.

12 March 2000, Salford 20–22 Warrington
This was a Challenge Cup quarter-final at The Willows and Warrington were on their way out of the competition as they trailed 20–18 as the tie approached its 5th minute of injury time. Centre Toa Kohe-Love then sent winger Alan Hunte racing over in the corner to steal a famous victory in front of the BBC TV cameras.

THE WIGAN WALK AND THE WIGAN RUN

There is no finer sight for a Warrington supporter than the Wigan walk, the process by which fans of the Cherry and Whites leave the ground en masse, 5 minutes early, when their favourites are heading for a certain defeat.

Warrington scrum-half Nathan Wood added to the genre with the Wigan run at The Halliwell Jones Stadium in May 2004. After dummying his way over for his second try of the night and making the score 20–0, the Australian ran into the stand and returned to the pitch from an opposite tunnel. On his travels apparently, he asked a Wigan supporter for a bite of his hot dog. Wood completed his hat-trick to earn the man-of-the-match award and Warrington won 34–18 after losing their previous 9 games against the Pie-eaters.

Another example of the friendly rivalry between Warrington and Wigan came in 2007 when The Halliwell Jones Stadium staged the Challenge Cup semi-final between Wigan and the Catalans Dragons. Hundreds of Warrington fans attended the match to cheer on the Dragons and were rewarded when the French team won 37–4 to reach the first final at the new Wembley.

HALL OF FAME

The Warrington Wolves Past Players' Association launched their Hall of Fame at a dinner in January 2003 when they inducted 12 founding members. Additional Hall of Famers have been added every year since then.

Founding members: Jack Arkwright, Brian Bevan, Jim Challinor, Billy Dingsdale, Jack Fish, Eric Fraser, Gerry Helme, Albert Johnson, Jack Miller, Harold Palin, Bill Shankland, Tommy Thompson.

2004:   Jim Featherstone, Laurie Gilfedder, Bob Ryan.

2005:   Willie Aspinall, Ernie Brookes, Frank Shugars.

2006:   Parry Gordon, Mike Gregory, Albert Naughton, George Thomas.

2007:   Harry Bath, Billy Cunliffe, Ken Kelly.

2008:   Ray Price, Jim Tranter, Derek Whitehead.

2009:   John Bevan, Dave Chisnall, Bobby Greenough,
        Arthur Skelhorn.

2010:   Kevin Ashcroft, Billy Holding, Alex Murphy.

2011:   Alf Boardman, Ronnie Duane, Tommy Martyn.

DREAM DEBUTS

Two Warrington wingers have scored 4 tries on their debuts. The first was Jason Roach, recently signed from Castleford, who raced in 4 times at Wakefield in a Challenge Cup fourth round tie in February 1998. Warrington, who were, of course, in the Super League, beat their First Division opponents 42–6.

Rob Smyth, on loan from London Broncos, repeated the feat in the Super League against the Huddersfield and Sheffield Giants at Wilderspool in July 2000, but, amazingly, finished on the losing side. Thanks to Smyth's 4 tries, Warrington built up a 20–0 lead in 24 minutes. Warrington were still ahead 24–6 at half time, but the second half belonged to the Giants who ran in 38 unanswered points to record a stunning 44–24 victory, their first at Wilderspool since March 1971 – 29 years earlier. Coach Darryl Van de Velde was devastated. 'We are just not good enough,' he said. 'Some of the blokes are just not up to Super League standard, they are First Division players. We had a poor training session on Friday. If you do not treat teams with respect they will come back and bite you on the bum and that's what happened today.'

More than 200 supporters staged a sit-down protest on the terraces after the match calling for Van de Velde to be sacked. After 45 minutes a tearful chief executive, Peter Deakin, emerged at the front of the main stand to apologise to them and assure them that things would be put right. So perhaps it wasn't a 'dream debut' after all.

Remarkably, Smyth was not the only Warrington player to score 4 tries in a match that season and still finish on the losing side. The same thing had happened to full-back Lee Penny at Leeds the previous month.

PLAYER OF THE 1940s – ALBERT JOHNSON (1939–51)

Adolf Hitler has a lot to answer for and he certainly made a mess of Albert Johnson's career. Johnson made his Warrington debut, aged 20, at home to Halifax in January 1939 but war broke out that September and Wilderspool was requisitioned by the military. Poor Albert ended up guesting for Wigan during the 1943/44 season, scoring 15 tries in 24 appearances. Once Hitler had been sorted out, Johnson could take his rightful place on Warrington's left wing where his pace and exquisite side-step helped him to score 112 tries in 198 appearances. His side-step, in fact, became the stuff of legend. On one occasion it is said that he was haring down the left wing at a packed Wilderspool, but being closed down rapidly by the opposing full-back. The full-back launched himself into a tackle but, in a fraction of a second, Johnson side-stepped out of reach, leaving the full-back to flatten an unfortunate touch judge. Johnson was Warrington's only representative on the Great Britain tour to Australia and New Zealand in 1946 and was a member of the side that won the Challenge Cup at Wembley in 1950, thrashing Widnes 19–0 in the final. His career came to a tragic end when he suffered a broken leg during the 1951 Championship Final against Workington Town in front of 61,618 fans at Maine Road. He never played again, but later served the club as a scout and spotted Brian Glover playing for Pilkington Recs. Glover, like

Johnson himself, went on to score more than 100 tries for
Warrington. Johnson died, aged 80, in 1998.

Appearances: 198
Tries: 112
Goals: 2
Points: 340

Honours: Challenge Cup 1949/50
Lancashire League 1947/48, 1948/49 and 1950/51.

MOST GOALS

Warrington's all-time leading goal-kickers (including drop
goals) are as follows:

1	Steve Hesford	1,159
2	Lee Briers	979
3	Billy Holding	834
4	Harry Bath	812
5	Derek Whitehead	734
6	Eric Fraser	473
7	Harold Palin	439
8	Laurie Gilfedder	426
9	Jeff Bootle	345
10	Ben Jolley	325

HAT-TRICK HEROES

Before Jason Roach came along the dreamiest of dream
debuts belonged to five Warrington players who scored
hat-tricks on their first appearances. Some went on to enjoy
wonderful careers in primrose and blue, others faded quickly
into obscurity.

Bill Stockley v Bradford at Wilderspool	October 1924
Islwyn 'Izzy' Davies at Leigh	March 1937
Bryn Knowelden v Salford at Wilderspool	December 1947
Bill Churm v Blackpool at Wilderspool	October 1964
Neil Kenyon v Barrow at Wilderspool	January 1990

MOST APPEARANCES

1	Brian Bevan	620
2	Parry Gordon	528 (plus 15 as a sub)
3	Jack Miller	526
4	Mark Forster	442 (plus 16 as a sub)
5	Gerry Helme	442
6	Jimmy Tranter	439
7	Billy Cunliffe	438
8	Alf Boardman	403
9	George Thomas	385
10	George Dickenson	375
11	Lee Briers	366 (plus 13 as a sub)

LOSING STREAKS

Warrington's worst run was 10 defeats in a row stretched over 2 seasons. The Wolves ended the 2008 campaign under coach James Lowes with 5 successive defeats and kicked off 2009 with another 5 losses as follows:

2008

9 August	St Helens	A	16–17	L
17 August	Hull KR	H	34–36	L
24 August	Castleford	A	24–44	L
6 September	Huddersfield	H	20–38	L
13 September	Catalans	A	8–46	L

2009

13 February	St Helens	A	14–26	L
21 February	Catalans	H	20–40	L
27 February	Wakefield	A	22–48	L
8 March	Leeds	H	14–20	L
14 March	Harlequins	A	8–60	L

The defeat at Catalans in September 2008 was in a play-off game while the other 9 defeats were in Super League matches. To halt the run of defeats, Tony Smith was appointed as head of rugby and coaching on 5 March. His second game in charge was the 60–8 thrashing at Harlequins, during which Australian centre Matt King made an offensive gesture to supporters who had been abusing him throughout the game. Things could only get better and did. Warrington beat Hull KR 24–12 at The Halliwell Jones Stadium the following week, their first win for 7 months, and have not looked back since.

FINAL MISERY

Warrington's Welsh scrum-half Dai Davies was lucky enough to play in four Challenge Cup finals, but unlucky enough to lose them all. He started the 1928 final on the wing, but reverted to his favourite scrum-half role following an injury to Billy Kirk. He was, however, powerless to prevent Warrington from losing 5–3 to Swinton at Central Park. Davies gave his finest performance in a Warrington shirt in the 1933 final at Wembley, capping a brilliant display with 2 tries in a heart-breaking 21–17 defeat to Huddersfield. Davies was sold to Huddersfield the following year and collected his third losers' medal with them in 1935. His fourth, as the Keighley captain, followed in 1937. Davies eventually lost his record as the biggest loser to the Great Britain centre Paul Loughlin who missed out with St Helens (1987, 1989, 1991) and Bradford Bulls (1996 and 1997).

Warrington prop Jack 'Cod' Miller played in the losing finals of 1928, 1933 and 1936, making him the only Wire player with three losers' medals from his time at the club. Miller finally got his hands on a winners' medal in 1945 while guesting for Huddersfield. That final was a two-legged affair against Bradford and Huddersfield won both legs, 7–4 at Fartown and 6–5 at Odsal.

PLAYER OF THE 1950S – BRIAN BEVAN (1945–62)

In the 1950s some misguided individuals thought the initials BB stood for the French actress Brigitte Bardot. How wrong they were. BB was Brian Bevan, the greatest winger in the history of rugby league. In brief, Bev scored a world record 796 tries including a club record 740 for Warrington in a club record 620 appearances. In his best season, 1952/53, he scorched in for 66 tries in 41 appearances and another club record that will probably never be broken. On two occasions he scored a club record 7 tries in a match, against Leigh in 1948 and against Bramley in 1953. He collected two Challenge Cup winners' medals (1950 and 1954) and three Championship winners' medals (1948, 1954 and 1955) and completed the set with the 1959 Lancashire Cup final win against St Helens when he scored the winning try. He also scored what came to be known as 'the try of the century' at Wigan in August 1948 in the traditional pre-season Wardonia Cup charity game. In front of 31,000 fans and with the scores tied at 5–5, Warrington were under intense pressure at a scrum 5 yards from their own line. The ball was fed out to Bevan who set off on a thrilling and bewildering 125-yard diagonal run, which would see him beat the entire Wigan team and touch down in the opposite corner. By 1961, the Warrington wingers – Bev and Terry O'Grady – had scored 1,000 career tries between them.

Oh, and just to add to the mix, Leeds had rejected him before he signed for Warrington, saying that he looked too skinny and feeble to be a rugby league player. Fellow Australian Bill Shankland, the former Warrington captain, then suggested that he try his luck at Wilderspool. When, in October 1988, the Rugby Football League instituted a Hall of Fame, Bevan was one of the founding members and when he died, aged 66, in June 1991, a generation of rugby league fans went into mourning. Two years later, a magnificent bronze statue of Bevan in full flight was officially unveiled on the Wilderspool Causeway roundabout and has since been relocated to The Halliwell Jones Stadium. Close by is the Brian Bevan Wall and together they form two permanent reminders of a unique talent.

Bevan's death was even recorded in parliament when Doug Hoyle, the Warrington North MP, tabled a House of Commons motion as follows: 'This House very much regrets the death of Brian Bevan, a legendary figure in rugby league. In the opinion of many he was the greatest winger to have graced the game and all sport will be poorer for his passing.'

Appearances: 620
Tries: 740
Goals: 34
Points: 2,288
Honours: Championship 1947/48, 1953/54 and 1954/55
Challenge Cup 1949/50 and 1953/54
Lancashire Cup 1959/60
Lancashire League 1947/48, 1948/49, 1950/51, 1953/54, 1954/55 and 1955/56
Television Trophy 1955/56.

GANG OF FOUR

Four Warrington players have played in four Challenge Cup finals for the club, each collecting two winners' and two losers' medals. Winger Jack Fish, centre Danny Isherwood and forward Alf Boardman all played in the winning sides of 1905 and 1907 and the losing sides of 1901 and 1904. Welsh forward George Thomas also featured in the winning sides of 1905 and 1907 but collected his losing medals in 1904 and 1913.

WINNING STREAKS

Warrington's best winning streak stretched to 21 victories, from April to November 1948, as follows:

1947/48

12 April	Halifax	A	9–3	W
17 April	Oldham	H	45–3	W
24 April	Huddersfield	H	17–5	W
8 May	Bradford	N	15–5	W

1948/49

21 August	Halifax	A	18–2	W
26 August	Liverpool	A	40–8	W
28 August	Bradford	A	19–7	W
4 September	Barrow	H	30–8	W
8 September	Barrow	A	7–4	W
11 September	Rochdale	A	17–7	W
16 September	Leigh	A	15–10	W
18 September	Leeds	H	39–17	W
25 September	Huddersfield	H	25–2	W
28 September	Oldham	H	55–0	W
2 October	Oldham	A	37–0	W
9 October	Whitehaven	H	48–15	W
11 October	Halifax	H	36–4	W
16 October	St Helens	A	12–4	W

23 October	Rochdale	H	15–6	W
30 October	Australia	H	16–7	W
6 November	Barrow	A	6–5	W

Not surprisingly, the 17 wins from 21 August to 6 November 1948 form Warrington's best-ever start to a season. During the record-breaking run, Warrington were crowned champions for the first time by beating Bradford Northern 15–5 at Maine Road, Manchester. During the 21 matches, Brian Bevan scored 32 tries while Harold Palin kicked 77 goals. Oldham were beaten three times – and on each occasion Bevan scored 5 tries.

Warrington's best run in the Super League – so far – is the 10 wins in a row under coach Tony Smith in 2011:

19 June	Hull KR	A	46–16	W
24 June	St Helens	H	35–28	W
1 July	Castleford	A	48–18	W
8 July	Huddersfield	H	28–16	W
16 July	Harlequins	A	54–24	W
31 July	Bradford	H	64–6	W
14 August	Wakefield	H	66–12	W
20 August	Catalans	A	25–12	W
4 September	Wigan	H	39–12	W
9 September	Hull	A	34–12	W

WAR HEROES

Anybody who fights for his king and country is a war hero in my book but here are two Warrington players who got medals to prove it. Jimmy Tilley, who was the full-back when

Warrington won the Challenge Cup in 1907, was awarded the Distinguished Conduct Medal in 1916 for 'conspicuous gallantry'. New Zealander Rex King, a fine loose-forward who made 76 appearances between 1934 and 1937, scoring 29 tries, won the Military Cross in 1942 for bravery on Crete.

MOST TRIES IN A SEASON

66	Brian Bevan	1952/53
62	Brian Bevan	1953/54
61	Brian Bevan	1954/55
60	Brian Bevan	1950/51
57	Brian Bevan	1947/48
56	Brian Bevan	1948/49
54	Brian Bevan	1958/59
53	Brian Bevan	1955/56
48	Brian Bevan	1946/47
46	Brian Bevan	1951/52
45	Brian Bevan	1957/58
40	Brian Bevan	1959/60
37	Bob Eccles	1982/83
35	Brian Bevan	1960/61
34	Islwyn 'Izzy' Davies	1938/39
33	Steve Ray	1932/33
32	Chris Hicks	2010
30	Brian Bevan	1949/50
30	Bobby Greenough	1960/61
30	John Bevan	1977/78
30	Joel Monaghan	2011

FIVE RECORD DEFEATS

17 January 1914, Hull 51–8 Warrington
Warrington's first team were on strike over the non-payment of a £1 bonus and so this was always going to get messy. The committee picked a reserve side instead and one of them, stand-off Alec Brown, suffered a dislocated collarbone after 15 minutes. Hull took full advantage, scoring 13 tries and kicking 6 goals. Brown never played for the first team again and was killed during the First World War.

10 April 1928, Hunslet 68–14 Warrington
Four days before the 1928 Challenge Cup final against Swinton at Central Park, Warrington sent a team full of youngsters to Parkside to face Hunslet and who could blame them? The Parksiders ran riot. Warrington were losing 35–0 at half time, conceded 16 tries in all and, to cap a miserable afternoon, prop Jack 'Cod' Miller was sent off, along with a Hunslet player, for fighting. The resulting defeat was a club record for 68 years. Warrington were later fined £15 for fielding a weakened team.

29 November 1970, Warrington 0–50 Salford
The great Parry Gordon was Warrington's scrum-half on this painful Sunday afternoon and would have nightmares about it for years to come. Full-back Derek Whitehead, another who would go on to achieve great things in the years to follow, was lucky; he missed the match through injury. Warrington were losing 29–0 at half time and went on to concede 12 tries in total on their way to a record home defeat. Jack Steel in the *Warrington Guardian* described it as the 'ultimate in demoralisation' and not surprisingly perhaps, some supporters forgot the game during the second half and turned their anger at the directors' box. After 32 minutes and with Warrington already losing 21–0, coach Peter Harvey sent on substitute forward Brian Brady, to replace Peter Cannon,

with the message, 'Go on, change the game.' Thanks coach. Maurice Richards scored 4 tries for Salford. David Watkins scored a try and kicked 7 goals.

3 January 1996, St Helens 80–0 Warrington
Amazingly, this was a Regal Trophy semi-final at Knowsley Road and a close contest was expected. It was also Paul Cullen's first game as Warrington captain. St Helens ran in 14 tries and Bobbie Goulding kicked 12 goals. The defeat was too much for coach Brian Johnson, a proud and intelligent man, to bear. He resigned the following day after 7 years in the post. He deserved a better fate. Goulding's son, Bobby, signed for Warrington, aged 15, in January 2009.

9 September 2001, Warrington 12–84 Bradford Bulls
Steve Anderson's brief reign as Warrington coach was not a barrel of laughs and this was the least funny episode of the lot; and it was all played out in front of Wilderspool's biggest crowd of the season – 8,393. Warrington had beaten Bradford 18–14 at Wilderspool the previous month under caretaker coach Paul Darbyshire and the Bulls were clearly out for revenge – and they got it. To add to the supporters' anger, there were suggestions that some of the Warrington players had been at a barbecue the night before and drinking alcohol. It remains Warrington's biggest Super League defeat. The aggregate total of 96 points is also the most ever scored in a league match involving Warrington.

SEVENTH HEAVEN

Here are seven record victories to savour:

30 December 1893, Warrington 59–0 Rugby
Take that rugby union, your boys took a hell of a beating. This was Rugby's last visit to Wilderspool and I don't think they enjoyed it. Warrington scored 13 tries (worth 3 points each)

and kicked 10 goals (worth 2 points each). Stand-off John Willie Evans led the rout with 2 tries and 7 goals while forward Will Nevins helped himself to a try and 3 goals. Centre Charley Potts claimed a hat-trick while his winger, Jack Massey, crossed twice as did forward James 'Buff' Berry. Will Randles, G. Dakin and Fair Barber (who was making his debut) also scored tries. To add to Rugby's embarrassment this was not even Warrington's best team because their three county players – half-backs James T. Bate and John T. Bate and forward James Jolley – were all playing for Lancashire against Cheshire at Fallowfield, Manchester, in the County Championship.

Warrington: Heesom; Massey, Potts, Barber, Carey; Evans, Clark; Turner, Nevins, Buckley, Donohue, Berry, Thorniley, Randles, Dakin.

12 April 1909, Warrington 78–6 St Helens
Easter Monday 1909 was to feature in Warrington's record books for the next 90 years following this record-breaking romp. St Helens arrived at Wilderspool with a weakened team and then lost a player with a broken leg, reducing them to 12 men, but the Wirepullers showed them no mercy. In front of 3,000 delighted spectators, Warrington were leading 40–0 at half time and went on to score 20 tries and kick 9 goals. If only their goal-kicking had been a little bit better they could easily have racked up 90 points. Winger Bert Bradshaw and Welsh forward George Thomas scored 5 tries apiece to equal Jack Fish's club record. Thomas also kicked 8 goals – 7 conversions and 1 from a mark – for a club record haul of 31 points. Jack Fish kicked one goal and scored a try. Some accounts wrongly credited Thomas with all 9 goals and 33 points, but whether he claimed 31 points or 33 points hardly matters. Either way it was a club record that stood for 90 years.

27 February 2000, Warrington 84–1 York
York had thrashed the Bradford amateurs Dudley Hill 56–10 in the third round but were given a taste of their own medicine

at Wilderspool. Stand-off Lee Briers led the way with a club record 40 points, made up of 3 tries and 14 goals, to overtake George Thomas. The 14 goals equalled Harold Palin's club record haul against Liverpool Stanley at Wilderspool in September 1950. Substitute forward Gary Chambers, hardly a prolific try-scorer, crossed twice as did Alan Hunte and Toa Kohe-Love as Warrington ran in 14 tries.

17 April 2006, Castleford 6–64 Warrington

Rugby league records can get complicated but this was Warrington's biggest away league win – because of the winning margin of 58 points – and remains the most points they have scored away from home in a league game. Again it was an Easter Monday and Lee Briers had a field day, scoring a try and kicking 10 goals. Warrington ran in 11 tries in total, including 3 in the last 7 minutes. Right wing Henry Fa'afili and his centre Martin Gleeson scored 2 tries each.

8 April 2011, Warrington 82–6 Harlequins

Harlequins arrived at The Halliwell Jones Stadium, like Warrington, with 4 wins from their opening 5 Super League matches, making this, in theory at least, a top-of-the-table clash. They headed back to London with their tails well and truly between their legs. Full-back Brett Hodgson led the romp with a try and 13 goals from 14 attempts for a 30-point haul. When he missed his thirteenth kick at goal, with the score already at 76–6, he received some good natured boos from Warrington fans who were clearly enjoying themselves. Chris Bridge scored a hat-trick inside 25 minutes.

22 April 2011, Salford 0–60 Warrington

This was Good Friday and what a *good* Friday it was as the Wolves chalked up the biggest away league win in their history, at least the biggest away winning margin in their history, of 60 points. Warrington scored 10 tries and the immaculate Brett Hodgson kicked all 10 conversions. Stand-off Lee Briers and winger Rhys Williams each crossed twice. The only blot on the afternoon was the fractured cheekbone suffered by 20-year-old scrum-half Richard Myler, a former Salford player. In terms of winning margin at least this win even overtook the record 68–10 thrashing of Chorley in the Regal Trophy in November 1995, although that remains the most points Warrington have scored in an away fixture.

20 May 2011, Warrington 112–0 Swinton Lions
This was great fun – unless, of course, you supported Swinton. Warrington were leading 48–0 at half time and ran in a record-equalling 20 tries in total. Lee Briers was at his sensational best, kicking a club record 16 goals, including some from the touchline, and scoring a hat-trick of tries. His 44-point haul smashed his own club record of 40 against York (above). The 44 points also took him past Steve Hesford's career points total of 2,416. Swinton, who were top of Championship One and unbeaten in their previous 12 matches, never stopped trying but were hopelessly outgunned.

CLEAN SHEETS

Warrington seemed to break points-scoring records for fun in 2011, but just as impressive was their mean-machine defence. They even achieved 3 consecutive clean sheets, something they had not done since 1904.

1904

12 March	Swinton 0–0 Warrington
16 March	Warrington 20–0 Swinton
19 March	Warrington 3–0 Wigan

All three games were Challenge Cup ties.

2011

7 May	Warrington 80–0 Keighley
13 May	Warrington 62–0 Castleford
20 May	Warrington 112–0 Swinton

The Keighley and Swinton games were in the Challenge Cup. The Castleford game was in the Super League.

WOLFING IT UP

Many supporters were unhappy when Warrington became the Warrington Wolves for the start of the 1997 season. After generations of being known as the Wire it seemed a little bit trite and unnecessary. However, the new club mascot Wolfie was an instant hit and soon won over most of the doubters. At first, changing the name did nothing to improve the fortunes of the team as shown at Bradford that March when the Bulls played 'Who's afraid of the big, bad wolf?' over the loud speakers on their way to a comfortable 58–20 victory. Warrington added to their wolf credentials in 2008 by adopting the Latin proverb 'lupus non mordet lupum' which translates literally to 'a wolf does not bite a wolf'. In other words, 'wolves stick together'.

NASTY NAZIS

Warrington's home game against Broughton Rangers on 14 September 1940 had barely finished when a German aircraft attacked the Thames Board Mills factory at Arpley Meadows, less than a mile from the ground. Centre Fred Higginbottom recalled, 'I was just getting in the bath and I thought the stand was going to fall in. Nobody expected it. Nobody knew what it was. I don't think we'd had a bomb before. It was terrifying.'

ON YOUR BIKE

It is bad enough losing players to injury, illness and suspension but Warrington have also lost them to emigration. Forward Tom Fell, who played in the 1901 Challenge Cup final, emigrated to South Africa the following year. He settled near Johannesburg and continued to play rugby.

Ball-playing prop Doug 'Nat' Silcock emigrated to Australia at the end of the 1960/61 season. Another forward, hooker and former captain Tony Miller, emigrated to Australia in February 1977. Likewise, centre Ian Sibbit moved to Melbourne Storm in 2001.

NEVER RELEGATED

One of Warrington's many proud boasts is that the team – unlike, say, Widnes and Wigan – have never been relegated. Also, unlike say, Leeds and St Helens, Warrington have always played in the top division. But even the most fanatical of supporters would have to admit that there has been an element of good fortune on both counts in that Warrington's worst seasons have occurred when there was only a single professional division, rather than two or even three. Warrington's worst league campaign was the 1970/71 season when the Wire finished 22nd out of the 30 clubs in the competition, below teams like Batley, Bramley and Barrow.

WORST STARTS TO THE SEASON

On two occasions, Warrington have lost their opening 5 games. The first was in that dreadful 1970/71 campaign. Look away now if you don't want to know the results.

1970/71

21 August	Wigan	H	11–17	L
28 August	Leigh	H	9–21	L
31 August	Widnes	H	11–16	L
4 September	Hull KR	A	9–20	L
9 September	Whitehaven	A	8–17	L

Warrington broke their duck with a 12–9 win at home to Huyton in front of just 1,893 fans.

The second 5-match losing streak at the start of a season came in 2009 and was part of the club record 10-match losing run, listed elsewhere.

PLAYER OF THE 1960s – PARRY GORDON (1963–81)

After the glory days of the late 1940s and '50s, the 1960s were a dark decade for Warrington but one player, above all others, made it bearable: scrum-half Parry Gordon. Signed on his 16th birthday in February 1961, he made his first-team debut at home to Barrow two years later. Pretty soon he was the club's first-choice scrum-half and remained so for the next 15 years. Most years he was either Warrington's captain, leading try-scorer or player of the season. His rewards came in the 1970s when he went to Wembley twice (1974 and 1975) and was a key member of the teams that won the Captain Morgan Trophy (1974), the Player's No. 6 Trophy (1974) and John Player Trophy (1978). On one memorable afternoon in March 1974 he scored 5 tries against Dewsbury, who were the rugby league champions at the time. He played 7 times for Lancashire and went on England's World Cup tour of Australia and New Zealand in 1975. However, he never played for Great Britain and that led to him frequently being described as the best ever uncapped scrum-half – a label he hated.

In recognition of his outstanding career, he was awarded not one, but two testimonial seasons by Warrington. When he finally hung up his boots in 1981, he had made 528 full appearances plus 15 as a substitute for the Wire, scoring 167 tries. Only Brian Bevan has played more games for the club. He later served as an assistant coach to both Billy Benyon and Kevin Ashcroft before stepping down to spend more time with his wife, Val, and three daughters. Former Warrington coach Alex Murphy described him as, 'The little man with the big heart.' Parry was inducted into the Warrington Wolves Hall of Fame in 2006 and his sudden death, aged 64, 3 years later, prompted an outpouring of grief from Warrington supporters.

Appearances: 528 + 15 as a substitute
Tries: 167
Goals: 1
Points: 503

Honours: Challenge Cup 1973/74
Club Championship 1973/74
Captain Morgan Trophy 1973/74
Player's No. 6 Trophy 1973/74
John Player Trophy 1977/78
Lancashire League 1967/68.

DOUBLE TROUBLE

Only a Warrington player could be sent off twice in the same match, even though he wasn't playing for Warrington at the time. His name was Jack Arkwright, he was a second-row forward, his friends called him Arky and he was on tour with Great Britain in Australia. The year was 1936, the opposition were Northern Districts and the venue was Armidale, New South Wales. History was about to be made.

Years later he recalled, 'I tackled one of their players a bit hard and another bloke burst up and jumped on me. I thumped him and the referee ordered me off. But their captain, possibly with revenge in mind, made a plea on my behalf and the referee relented. After taking more stick and with only two minutes of the match remaining I thumped their captain. The referee spotted me. "All right," I said. "I'm going this time." And I walked.'

Three days later Arkwright was sent off again, after laying out the Australian prop Ray Stehr (a policeman by trade) in the third Test between the Kangaroos and Great Britain at the Sydney Cricket Ground. A brass band played 'Goodnight Sweetheart' as he left the field. When, eventually, he was revived, Stehr was sent off too.

As mentioned elsewhere, Arkwright made his final appearance for Warrington in 1945, aged 42, for a club record that is unlikely to be beaten. He was not a huge fan of the modern game. 'It's just like tick rugby. It just gets on my nerves people not tackling properly.'

TWO FOND FAREWELLS

23 April 1962, Brian Bevan

All good things must come to an end and so even the great Brian Bevan's career had to finish sometime. In June 1961 he had celebrated his 37th birthday and, during the 1961/62 season that followed, he had been dropped on a couple of occasions, particularly when the grounds were thick with mud. Finally, it was decided that he would leave the club at the end of the season and make a farewell appearance against Leigh at Wilderspool on Easter Monday 1962. The afternoon that followed was emotional and triumphant. Warrington's biggest crowd of the season – 16,578 – turned up to say goodbye and Bevan was made captain for the day on his 620th appearance for the first team. The occasion, of course, demanded a farewell try and that arrived after 10 minutes when stand-off Bobby Greenough made a break and 'Bev' was backing up, ready to take the pass and score. It was his 740th try in primrose and blue. More drama followed when, in the last minute, Greenough went over for his second try of the afternoon to make the score 29–17 and handed the ball to Bevan. The great Australian placed the ball professionally, took aim and sent his kick soaring towards the posts. Sadly, the ball drifted wide. The final whistle blew seconds later and Bevan was carried off the pitch on the shoulders of his team-mates while the applauding Leigh players formed a guard of honour. Even as he disappeared into the tunnel the fans started chanting 'We want Bev' and he came out into the centre of the main stand as the crowd sang 'For he's a jolly good fellow' and 'Waltzing Matilda'. There wasn't a dry eye in the house.

21 September 2003, Wilderspool

The final Super League game at Wilderspool before the move to The Halliwell Jones Stadium was another emotionally charged occasion. Wakefield Trinity Wildcats were the visitors and all Warrington had to do to reach the Super League play-offs for the first time was avoid defeat. On a memorable afternoon, however, the Wolves did much, much more than that to romp home 52–12. Stand-off Graham Appo led the way with a hat-trick of tries and 10 goals from 10 attempts for a 32-point haul. Super Sid Domic scored the 8th and final try deep into injury time to bring the house down. Coach Paul Cullen addressed the fans afterwards from the centre of the pitch to thank the team for a performance that, he said, did justice to the memory of all the great players who had played there. A Super League record crowd for Wilderspool – 9,944 – savoured every moment.

The final competitive match at Wilderspool was staged the following month against the touring New Zealand 'A' team when a depleted Warrington side, led by the Australian

Darren Burns and with 11 young players making their debuts, won 28–26. Unlike the Wakefield game, this was a low-key affair, watched by just 3,409 supporters, and after the final hooter, the Warrington Pipe Band played 'Auld Lang Syne'.

WHAT WARRINGTON HAVE WON

7 Challenge Cups
9 Lancashire Cups
3 Championships
2 League Leaders Trophies
1 Club Championship
1 Premiership Trophy
1 Captain Morgan Trophy
8 Lancashire League titles
1 Player's No. 6 Trophy
2 John Player Trophies
1 Regal Trophy
2 South West Lancashire and Border Towns Trophies
1 Television Trophy
1 British Coal Nines
1 Wigan Sevens

VALUE FOR MONEY

Full-back David Lyon was the first player Warrington signed where the fee was fixed by a Rugby League Tribunal. This was back in the summer of 1987 and Lyon was out of contract at Widnes. Warrington had offered £10,000 but Widnes were asking for £20,000. The tribunal – sitting on Tuesday 1 September – valued him at £12,500. At Wilderspool, Lyon developed into such a fine player that Warrington were able to sell him to St Helens five years later for £90,000 – a then record fee for a full-back.

FIGHT CLUB

A number of Warrington players have fancied their chances at the noble art of boxing, with varying degrees of success. Winger Elliot Harris (1898–1906) boxed throughout South West Lancashire. Welsh forward Arthur 'Candy' Evans (1931–4) was the amateur heavyweight champion of Wales but enjoyed less success as a professional. In May 1932, he fought Ireland's Jack Doyle at London's Crystal Palace, but the bout only lasted 2 minutes. After Evans had scored with two light lefts, the Irishman knocked him out with a heavy right to the jaw. Prop Adam Fogerty (1998) was also a heavyweight and had the impressive record of 18 wins from 19 fights before taking up rugby league. At one time he was ranked number three in England and number five in Europe. However, he threw his most famous punch in January 1995 during an episode of *Coronation Street* when, as the hit man, he thumped Jack Duckworth, apparently mistaking him for his brother Cliff.

GRAPPLE TACKLES

A couple of Warrington players have also been professional wrestlers. Winger Tommy Blinkhorn (1928–33) was the first but Frank Gregory (1938–46) was the most famous. He had been the amateur heavyweight wrestling champion of Cornwall before taking up rugby league and wrestled professionally when his rugby career was over. On Monday 20 October 1958, he took part in a contest at Warrington Baths, which was promoted in the usual enthusiastic manner; 'Francis St Clair Gregory (Redruth). The ex-Warrington and Wigan prop-forward, eight times Cornish champion; one of the roughest mat men in the game' was pitted against 'Massambula (West Africa). The only wrestling witch doctor.' Gregory was disqualified in the fifth round for persistent fouling.

GREAT BRITAIN CALLING

In the days before mobile phones, text messages and even Teletext, Warrington captain Willie Aspinall found out that he had been selected for the 1966 Great Britain tour of Australia and New Zealand during a match at Whitehaven one Wednesday afternoon that March when a message was passed on to the pitch. 'During the game our winger Brian Glover ran across the pitch and threw me in the air, congratulating me on being picked,' said Aspinall. The stand-off proved to be a fine tourist, scoring 10 tries in 17 full appearances plus 3 as a substitute.

Prop or second-row forward Paul Wood was one of Warrington's best players in the 2003 season but even he did not expect a call from Great Britain coach David Waite asking him to join the squad to face Australia that November. 'At first I thought it was a prank call and that Nathan Wood was back in town, that's his sort of style. But I'm absolutely delighted,' said Wood, then 22. Sadly, however, he suffered a shoulder injury in the warm-up game against New Zealand 'A' at Headingley that ruled him out of the Ashes series.

Alex Murphy won his 27th and final Great Britain cap in October 1971, 5 months into his 7-year reign as Warrington coach. Murphy, then 32, lined up against New Zealand at Castleford, alongside a young hooker by the name of Mike 'Stevo' Stephenson, who made his GB debut that day as a substitute forward. Murphy had won his previous 26 caps while at St Helens.

Welsh forward George Thomas was the first Warrington player to represent Great Britain – or the Northern Union as they were known at the time – against New Zealand at Chelsea's Stamford Bridge ground in the second Test on Saturday 8 February 1908. Great Britain lost 18–6.

Loose-forward Mike Gregory is Warrington's most capped Great Britain international with 20 between 1987 and 1990 from 19 starting appearances plus 1 as a substitute. But John

Bevan is the club's most capped international, with 23, from 6 Great Britain caps and 17 Welsh caps – just ahead of prop Billy Cunliffe who won 11 Great Britain caps and 10 England caps – with Gregory in third place.

GREAT BRITAIN TOURISTS

1910	Frank Shugars
1920	Billy Cunliffe, Arthur Skelhorn
1924	Billy Cunliffe, Edmund Osborne (manager)
1928	Edmund Osborne (manager)
1932	Billy Dingsdale, Bob Anderton (manager)
1936	Jack Arkwright, Jack Miller, Bob Anderton (manager)
1946	Albert Johnson
1950	Jim Featherstone, Bob Ryan
1954	Gerry Helme, Ray Price
1958	Jim Challinor, Eric Fraser
1962	Eric Fraser, Laurie Gilfedder
1966	Willie Aspinall
1974	Kevin Ashcroft, John Bevan
1979	Tommy Martyn
1984	Ronnie Duane
1988	Mike Gregory
1990	Mike Gregory (captain), Dave Lyon (replacement)
1992	Kevin Ellis
1996	Iestyn Harris, Jonathan Roper, Paul Sculthorpe

The 1950 tourists were the last to travel to Australia by boat, meaning that Jim Featherstone and Bob Ryan had to miss the Challenge Cup final against Widnes at Wembley.

HOLE IN ONE

Australian forward Simon Gillies (1999) achieved a hole in one at Walton Hall Golf Club during his one-season stay at Wilderspool. However, the best golfer – and probably the best all-round sportsman – ever to play for Warrington was another Australian, the legenday Bill Shankland. When Shankland signed for Warrington in 1931, he did so in the hope of furthering his golfing career and, in the days when rugby league players were very much part-time, he was able to pursue both sports. In 1939, he finished joint third in the Open Championship at St Andrews, the home of golf, and followed that by finishing fourth at Royal Liverpool in 1947 and tying for sixth place at Royal Portrush, Northern Ireland, in 1951. Later, as the golf professional at the Potters Bar club in Hertfordshire he moulded the career of a brash, young, Tony Jacklin, who became Open champion in 1969.

Shankland made his last appearance at Wilderspool in September 1998, aged 91, as the star turn in a parade of past players to mark the ground's centenary. Tragically, at his hotel the following day, he slipped and fell, banging his head and never regained consciousness.

UNITED WE STAND

Over the years, Warrington have had a number of links with Manchester United. Warrington's first professional trainer, appointed in September 1910 after the club placed a newspaper advert, was a man called Fred Paley, a former professional sprinter from Sheffield. He had been training football teams for two decades and his CV included Carlisle United, Port Vale, Arsenal, Reading and Newton Heath (before they became Manchester United in 1902).

Warrington went one step further in September 1919 when they signed a Manchester United player. His name was Joe

Haywood and at United he was a half-back – a midfield player in modern terms – and had made 26 first-team appearances from November 1913 to April 1915. During the First World War, he started to play rugby league and enjoyed it. He played on the right wing for Warrington, scoring three tries in 22 appearances, before being transferred to Widnes.

Full-back Eric Fraser (1951–64) had a trial with Manchester United as did loose-forward Austin Heathwood (1949–58).

Warrington also played at Old Trafford in the 1987 Premiership final against Wigan. The game attracted a Premiership record crowd of 38,756 but an injury-hit Warrington side lost 8–0, with Joe Lydon scoring a long-range kick-and-run try.

FOOTBALL CRAZY

Wilderspool and The Halliwell Jones Stadium have both staged men's and women's football matches. On 13 October 1921, the unofficial England women's football team visited Wilderspool. They were known as Dick, Kerr's Ladies after the Preston munitions factory where the women worked during the First World War. They wore characteristic black and white hooped bobble hats – and they were good. At Wilderspool, they took on a team from Farnworth (Bolton) and won 11–0 despite the long grass hindering their skilful style of play. The game attracted a crowd of 4,000 and raised funds for the Warrington branch of the Royal British Legion. In 2005, The Halliwell Jones Stadium staged matches in the Women's European Championship.

On 2 November 1940, Wilderspool staged a friendly football international of sorts between England and Poland to raise money for charity. It was organised by officers of the United States Air Force based at Burtonwood Air Base and Poland won 3–2.

Liverpool reserves were based at The Halliwell Jones Stadium for two seasons from 2007 to 2009. On 26 February 2008, a record crowd of 10,546 turned out to see them take on Manchester United reserves.

Warrington have also played at many football grounds, including Anfield (Liverpool), Brunton Park (Carlisle), Craven Cottage (Fulham), Griffin Park (Brentford), Loftus Road (QPR), Maine Road (Manchester City), Old Trafford (Manchester United) and The Valley (Charlton).

CRIKEY, KIKEY!

Welsh centre Jesse Meredith (1927–31) was, by all accounts, a bit of an oddball. He preferred to be known by his nickname Kikey than his Christian name Jesse. Perhaps he had been called a big Jessie in his youth? Also, after signing from Abertillery, he pretended to his new team-mates that he could speak fluent Welsh when, in fact, he could do nothing of the sort. Kikey's kidology was finally exposed when Warrington signed another Welshman, scrum-half Dai Davies, whose first language was Welsh.

TOP DRAWS

Draws are relatively rare in rugby league but not unheard of. Players used to receive winning pay for an away draw and losing pay for a home draw. In the early days of the Northern Union, Warrington shared lots of 0–0 draws – including 6 in the 1896/97 season. The home and away league matches with Wigan both finished pointless. The team's last 0–0 draw was against Salford at The Willows in December 1974 in the BBC2 Floodlit Trophy final. Warrington lost the replay at Wilderspool 10–5. The highest scoring draw that Warrington have been involved in was the 30–30 tie with St Helens at

Wilderspool in June 2003. Warrington were trailing 30–24 when full-back Lee Penny powered his way over at the posts and Lee Briers added the conversion. The Warrington captain was then just off target with a drop goal attempt from the half-way line.

NARROWEST DEFEAT

Warrington's narrowest defeat was the 1–0 reverse at home to Workington in November 1979. Despite heavy rain, scrum-half Arnie Walker kicked a well-taken drop goal for Town while the normally reliable Steve Hesford missed three kickable penalties.

NO PLACE LIKE HOME

The tunnel to the changing rooms at Wilderspool was dug out in 1934 by four players who used to be miners before signing for the club.

Groundsman Jackie Hamblett, who held the post for 60 years, was the first man to mark 10-yard lines parallel to the touchlines at Wilderspool to help referees indicate where a scrum should form after a kick to touch. His idea was soon adopted by the Rugby Football League.

Warrington's best home campaign was in the 1953/54 season when the Wire won all 23 games they played at Fortress Wilderspool. The total was made up of 18 league games, two Challenge Cup ties, two Lancashire Cup ties and a Championship play-off semi-final.

Warrington played 9 consecutive home games between 1 February and 4 April 1947 as the rest of the country fell foul of arctic weather conditions.

WE ARE THE CHAMPIONS

Warrington have been crowned champions three times, each time at Manchester City's former Maine Road ground.

8 May 1948, Warrington 15–5 Bradford Northern
Warrington had lost three Championship Finals (1926, 1935 and 1937) before this one, but captained by local lad Harold Palin, who kicked 3 goals, the Wire finally put things right in front of a crowd of 69,143. No bull and no Bulls. Bradford were still called Bradford Northern at the time. Tries by Brian Bevan, Albert Pimblett and Stan Powell sealed the victory for a side coached by Welshman Emlyn Jenkins, the former Salford stand-off. The match was a personal triumph for Dave Cotton, aged 39, the Warrington hooker, who had won a Championship Final with St Helens in 1932 – 16 years earlier. Cotton won the scrum battle 36–28 to give Warrington more of the ball. The *Warrington Guardian* produced two souvenir booklets – one with a primrose cover and one with a blue cover – and both are much sought after by programme collectors.

8 May 1954, Warrington 8–7 Halifax
Warrington completed their first – and so far only – league and cup double with this victory. Four penalty goals from Harry Bath were the difference between the sides but the match is best remembered for a wrongly disallowed try by Brian Bevan. The Wire were on the attack and winger Stan McCormick booted the ball across the field to Bevan. The referee turned to watch the ball land and saw Bevan collecting it and touching down near the posts. He disallowed the score because he simply could not believe that any player could have got to the ball so quickly and still been on side which, of course, Bevan was. Full-back Eric Frodsham, standing in for the injured Albert Naughton, received the trophy.

14 May 1955, Warrington 7–3 Oldham
This was a pulsating match with both teams producing quality play, despite the fact that the pitch was wet and muddy due to heavy rain on the Friday and Saturday morning. The bad weather kept the attendance down to 49,434. There was also a hailstorm just before half time. Both teams changed their kits at the interval, but were soon just as muddy as they had been minutes before. Brian Bevan – Oldham's bogeyman – scored Warrington's try while Harry Bath kicked 2 crucial goals. Albert Naughton collected the trophy from the Earl of Derby after missing out the year before because of injury.

CHAMPIONS FOR 19 HOURS

Sky TV could have written the script for the end of the 1993/94 season. Three teams – Warrington, Bradford Northern and Wigan – went into the final weekend level on points at the top of the Stones Bitter Championship with one match left to play. Warrington would entertain Sheffield Eagles, Bradford would travel to Leeds and Wigan would go to Oldham. Warrington were first up on Friday 22 April and in front of a passionate crowd and with chants of 'Brian Johnson's barmy army' booming out from the Fletcher Street End, the Wire turned on the style to win 36–18. Tries from Greg Mackey, Rowland Phillips, Iestyn Harris, Jonathan Davies, Allan Bateman and Jonathan Roper made Warrington feel like champions, but only for 19 hours, until Bradford thrashed a weakened Leeds side 52–8 the following day. Wigan completed the job with a 50-6 victory at Oldham on the Sunday, condemning Warrington to third place on points difference.

Warrington: Davies; Forster, Bateman, Roper, Harris; Ellis, Mackey; Tees, Thursfield, Phillips, Darbyshire, Sanderson, Shelford. Subs: Bennett, Hilton.

MOST GOALS IN A SEASON

170	Steve Hesford	1978/79
162	Derek Whitehead	1973/74
162	Harry Bath	1952/53
158	Steve Hesford	1977/78
154	Harry Bath	1955/56
153	Harry Bath	1953/54
152	John Woods	1987/88
147	Steve Hesford	1980/81
146	Harold Palin	1948/49
142	Steve Hesford	1983/84

LEAGUE VERSUS UNION

The Second World War brought a ceasefire in the battle between rugby league and rugby union – there were more important things to worry about. In fact, there were two Rugby League versus Rugby Union games – both played under union rules – to raise money for services charities. Warrington's Welsh forward Bill Chapman played in both. The first, at Headingley, was between the Northern Command League XV and the Northern Command Union XV in 1943 and the RL side won 18–11. The second was at Odsal the following year and again the league side won, this time 15–10. Chapman was a private at the time of the first match but had been promoted to the rank of sergeant in time for the second encounter.

PLAYER OF THE 1970s –
JOHN BEVAN (1973–86)

For the generation of Warrington fans who started watching the Wire in the 1970s, like me, John Bevan was the swashbuckling hero. From his debut against Castleford in

September 1973 until his last appearance against Oldham in February 1986, Bevan could usually be relied upon to score a match-winning try or make a match-saving tackle and he always looked like he was enjoying himself.

The ultimate symbol of his job satisfaction, however, was the clenched fist salute with which he celebrated his tries, starting at Leigh on Boxing Day 1973. 'I intercepted a ball on the halfway line and no one was in front of me,' Bevan recalled in his testimonial brochure 10 years later. 'I realised I was going to score for the first time in ages and out of frustration came delight. Up went the arm.' It became his trademark and the fans loved it, although coach Alex Murphy vowed he would chop the arm off if the salute ever caused him to drop the ball in the act of scoring. Thankfully, it never did.

Bevan scored 4 tries that Boxing Day afternoon to signal his arrival as a genuine rugby league player after just 13 weeks in his new code. The following 6 months were the stuff of fairytales, with Bevan collecting four winners' medals (Captain Morgan Trophy, Player's No. 6 Trophy, Challenge Cup and Club Championship), playing at Wembley, being selected for the tour of Australia and New Zealand and winning the first of his 6 Great Britain caps.

The 1974/75 season was almost as good, with Bevan scoring a try at Wembley in the opening minutes of the Challenge Cup final against Widnes and making the first of 17 appearances for the reborn Welsh national side. It was too good to last, however, and it took Bevan another 8 years to earn his next four winners' medals (two for John Player Trophy successes and two for Lancashire Cup wins), although the tries and the memories kept piling up.

As the seasons rolled by, Bevan was increasingly used as a centre, a loose-forward and even a stand-off. His speed and, in particular, his strength made him a formidable opponent anywhere. At St Helens in September 1979, for example, Bevan began the match on the left wing and was switched to the loose-forward slot after Warrington had stand-off Ken

Kelly sent off and lost prop Steve Hogan and No. 13 Mike Peers with injuries. Bevan finished the afternoon with 4 tries and winning pay.

'Sleeves rolled up, socks down to his ankles, Bevan looked more like one of the Bash Street Kids and caused mayhem wherever he went,' wrote Robert Gate in *Gone North – Volume II*. 'Muscular, bursting with power and energy, Bevan simply epitomised aggression and determination.'

Those qualities had already seen Bevan play on the wing for Cardiff, Wales, the British Lions and the Barbarians before he joined Warrington in September 1973, one month short of his 23rd birthday. Best of all for Wire fans, in November 1972, Bevan had rejected the chance to join Wigan – a Warrington hero indeed.

Appearances: 331 + 1 as a substitute
Tries: 201
Goals: 7
Points: 628

Honours: Challenge Cup 1973/74
Club Championship 1973/74
Captain Morgan Trophy 1973/74
Player's No. 6 Trophy 1973/74
John Player Trophy 1977/78 and 1980/81
Lancashire Cup 1980/81, 1982/83.

INJURY TIME

Rugby league is a rough, tough and sometimes brutal sport and Warrington players have received some horrible injuries. Scrum-half Billy Kirk was felled by a rabbit punch during the 1928 Challenge Cup final and was carried off on a stretcher. Two men walking beside the stretcher had distinctive collars on their shirts and a rumour started that they were priests about to read Kirk his last rites. Thankfully, the rumours were false but Warrington were reduced to 12 men for the remaining half-hour.

In November 1922, George Lloyd suffered a badly broken leg during an 'A' team game at Wilderspool. The bone was broken in two places. Most people in the ground heard the bone crack and two or three people fainted.

Brilliant winger Albert Johnson suffered a broken leg 20 minutes into the 1951 Championship Final against Workington Town at Maine Road and never played again.

Cumbrian forward Dave Elliott broke his leg while playing for Warrington in an Alliance game in August 1995. Bone marrow got into his bloodstream and he ended up fighting for his life on a life support machine. He pulled through but, at the age of 24, was never to play again, although he did become a well-respected coach.

Forward Bob Eccles suffered two broken arms during the 1986/87 season. Winger Elliot Harris suffered two broken collarbones during the 1903/04 campaign. Stand-off Ken Kelly suffered a broken jaw – the second of his career – in a collision with Bradford Northern's Len Casey in May 1979. The injury ruled him out of Great Britain's tour of Australia and New Zealand that summer and did nothing for the Lions' chances of regaining the Ashes.

Players also get injured away from the pitch and the training field. Scrum-half Paul Bishop missed the 1990 Challenge Cup semi-final against Oldham after suffering a badly cut hand in a fall through a glass door at home on the morning of the match.

Warrington forward Jim Fearnley went to court in August 1914 after suffering a bizarre injury in a pub. Fearnley had ordered a pint of herb beer at the premises on Bewsey Street but suffered a cut hand when the handle came off while he was drinking it. Fearnley had to have stitches at Warrington Infirmary and take three weeks off work. Fearnley took the landlord to the County Court to claim damages and was awarded £4 11s plus costs.

Jack 'Cod' Miller (1926–46) fractured a forearm when using a starting handle to start a car in March 1927.

BEST OF ENEMIES

Allan Langer and Tawera Nikau were friends and team-mates at Warrington but also, of course, an Australian and a Kiwi. Their friendly rivalry continued into their respective retirements. When Nikau lost a leg in a motorcycle accident in 2003, Langer sent him a present to cheer him up: a pair of socks. Nikau thought it was hilarious.

LONGEST MATCH

The longest match played at Wilderspool was the 1915 Challenge Cup semi-final between St Helens and Rochdale Hornets – an epic contest that attracted a crowd of 10,000. The scores were level at 5–5 after 80 minutes and so, following a new rule designed to end the need for replays, a further 15 minutes each way were played. There were no further scores and so despite playing for 110 minutes they had to do it all over again at Central Park.

Warrington's longest match was the Challenge Cup quarter-final at Hull KR in 2009 that went into golden point extra time. Lee Briers kicked the winning drop goal in the 85th minute.

SHORTEST MATCH

Warrington's shortest match was the league fixture at St Helens in February 1990 which was abandoned after 4 minutes when a piece of roofing fell off the stand and frighteningly close to Wire centre Gary Mercer.

LANCASHIRE LADS

Modern-day supporters must wonder what all the fuss is about, after all Warrington has been a part of Cheshire since local government reorganisation in 1974. But before that Warrington was part of Lancashire and the Lancashire Cup was a much-loved competition and one the Wire won nine times. Here are the stories of the successful finals.

3 December 1921, Warrington 7–5 Oldham
Warrington lost centre Charlie Collins with a dislocated shoulder and, in the days before substitutes, had to play for 53 minutes with 12 men, but still won. Winger Bob Bradbury scored the only try while full-back Ben Jolley kicked 2 goals.

23 November 1929, Warrington 15–2 Salford
Winger Tommy Blinkhorn scored 1 of the 3 tries, meaning that he had scored a try in every round. Full-back Billy Holding, as well as having a fine game in open play, kicked 3 goals.

19 November 1932, Warrington 10–9 St Helens
Warrington had beaten Wigan in the semi-final and saw off Saints in front of a crowd of 28,500 at Central Park in the final. Tries from Dai Davies and Tommy Thompson plus two goals from Holding settled a thrilling contest.

23 October 1937, Warrington 8–4 Barrow
Warrington had prop Jack 'Cod' Miller sent off for dissent after 8 minutes but were inspired by captain Jack Arkwright. Two tries from Australian centre Dave Brown and a Bill Shankland conversion did the rest.

31 October 1959, Warrington 5–4 St Helens
This was billed as the battle of the two great wingers: Warrington's Australian veteran, Brian Bevan, aged 35,

against the South African Tom van Vollenhoven of St Helens, in his prime at 24. Bevan scored the match-winning try, beating van Vollenhoven to the touchdown in front of 39,237 supporters.

29 October 1965, Warrington 16–5 Rochdale Hornets
Played under floodlights at Knowsley Road on a Friday night this game attracted a crowd of 21,360. Two tries from Warrington centre Jackie Melling were the difference between the sides. Captain Jeff Bootle kicked 2 goals.

4 October 1980, Warrington 26–10 Wigan
Second Division Wigan fancied their chances, at least until Warrington opened up a 17–2 lead in the opening 18 minutes. Steve Hesford kicked a 1st-minute penalty and, from the restart, Tommy Martyn collected the ball and charged 60 yards to score in the corner. Unsung hero Tony Waller, the Wire hooker, was the man of the match.

23 October 1982, Warrington 16–0 St Helens
Easy peasy after tries from wingers Paul Fellows and Mike Kelly, both set up by man-of-the-match Steve Hesford, had put Warrington in command. Young guns Paul Cullen and Mike Gregory collected their first winners' medals. Veteran prop Dave Chisnall came on as a sub.

14 October 1989, Warrington 24–16 Oldham
Warrington had done the hard part by beating world club champions Widnes in the semi-final 4 days earlier but Second Division Oldham, coached by Tony Barrow, proved tough nuts to crack. Two tries from Bob Jackson earned him the man-of-the-match award.

In keeping with the Lancashire lads theme, 90 Warrington players represented Lancashire in the now-defunct County Championship – including Welshmen John Bevan and George Thomas. Please don't ask me to explain the thinking behind that. Prop Billy Cunliffe made the most Lancashire appearances (19) but winger Jack Fish scored the most tries, 16 in 16 appearances.

MR RELIABLE AND FRIENDS

Warrington captain Greg Mackey wrote his name into the club's record books by making 98 consecutive appearances from August 1992 until February 1995 when he was finally beaten by a persistent shoulder injury. But even that monumental feat of endurance only tells half of the story because his remarkable run had started with 94 consecutive appearances at his previous club Hull from November 1989. In total, then, the Australian scrum-half made 192 consecutive starts.

Mackey broke Steve Hesford's club record of 94 games in a row, set between October 1977 and December 1979. Hesford, however, still holds the record for scoring in consecutive games, 71, from October 1977 to May 1979.

Hooker Duane Mann would have beaten both Mackey and Hesford but for the fact that his 103 consecutive appearances from September 1990 to April 1993 included one appearance as a substitute at Rochdale in 1991. Sorry Duane, but rules are rules.

Australian wing Chris Hicks broke new ground in 2008 when he became the first Warrington player to play and score in every match in a season. Hicks scored 19 tries and kicked 79 goals in the 30 matches that year to clock up 234 points. Full-back Eric Frodsham holds the record for most appearances in a season – 48 – and he did it twice, in 1950/51 and again in 1953/54.

PLAYERS OF THE 1980s –
MIKE GREGORY (1982–94)

Great players produce brilliant performances when it matters most and Mike Gregory could be relied upon to do just that for both Warrington and Great Britain. No Great Britain fan over the age of 40 will ever forget the magnificent try that 'Greg' scored in the epic third Test victory over Australia at the Sydney Football Stadium in July 1988.

The Warrington captain was sent clear by his namesake Andy Gregory on Britain's 25-yard line and raced 70 yards to the posts, pursued in vain by Kangaroo skipper Wally Lewis and loose-forward Wayne Pearce. The try sealed a famous 26–12 victory and gave international rugby league a much-needed shot in the arm.

Two years later, Gregory scored another important try at another famous venue when he touched down for Warrington against Wigan in the Challenge Cup final at Wembley. A minute before half time, Gregory came storming on to an inside pass from scrum-half Paul Bishop to score at the posts and keep Warrington in contention at 16–8. This time he would finish on the losing side, but not before he had strained every sinew against his hometown club and created a second Warrington try for full-back David Lyon.

Gregory had joined Warrington from the Wigan St Patrick's amateur club in June 1982 and quickly established himself in the first team, collecting a Lancashire Cup winners' medal against St Helens in only his tenth appearance.

Gregory's enthusiasm on his debut that September is still fondly remembered, with the 18-year-old tackling player after player, to the delight of team-mates and supporters alike. He had to wait 4 years for his next winners' medal, against Halifax in the Premiership Trophy success of 1986, but that Elland Road afternoon signalled the start of four glorious seasons for club and country. Gregory captained Warrington to victory in the 1989 Lancashire Cup final and led the Lions to back-to-back series victories over the Kiwis, home and away, that same season.

Sadly, the non-stop playing schedule and 100 per cent commitment took its toll and Gregory spent more of the next 4 years on the treatment table than the pitch. A £35,000 transfer to Salford in 1994 did not change his luck and so Gregory began his coaching career, as assistant to Shaun McRae, at St Helens in April 1996. More success followed.

Gregory also had spells in charge of Swinton, the Great Britain Academy side and Wigan Warriors. Tragically, an insect bite led to him contracting a fatal and debilitating form of motor neurone disease and he died, aged 43, in November 2007. Warrington named the approach road to The Halliwell Jones Stadium Mike Gregory Way in his honour.

Appearances 222 + 24 as a substitute
Tries 45
Points 176
Honours: Premiership Trophy 1985/86
Lancashire Cup 1982/83 and 1989/90.

TALL AND SHORT

Rugby league players are getting taller all the time – you can almost hear them growing. So the tallest player in the club's history is probably the 6ft 4in Australian centre Matt King, who was even taller with his curly, afro hairstyle. The shortest player in the club's history is probably the half-back D.H. Edmunds (1902–3) who was barely 5ft tall and was known as 'Little Tich' after the music hall comedian Harry Relph.

FAT AND THIN

As rugby league players get taller and taller they are also getting heavier and heavier. It stands to reason. But James 'Tosh' Thorniley, whose career spanned the club's rugby union and rugby league days, was ahead of his time. In the 1890s he weighed more than 16 stones and that made him a formidable scrummager. Fast forward to 1995 and the Australian prop Dave King weighed in at 19st 3lb. Scrum-half Frank Cueto (1936–40) was at the other end of the scales. When he signed for Warrington, aged 19, from Maryport in Cumberland in March 1936, he weighed just 9 stones. Modern-day players would snap him in half like a twig.

CUP KINGS

Warrington have won the Challenge Cup, rugby league's most glamorous prize, seven times and every success was special for the players and supporters involved.

29 April 1905, Warrington 6–0 Hull KR
After losing the 1901 and 1904 finals, this was a case of third time lucky for the Wirepullers. Winger Jack Fish, who had played in both of those defeats, scored both the tries at Headingley. Fish himself missed the first conversion while captain Jack Hallam hit the posts with the second. In the end it didn't matter, Warrington had finally won the cup.

27 April 1907, Warrington 17–3 Oldham
By now, Jack Fish was the captain and he led his team to victory at Wheater's Field, Broughton with a sensational try and 4 goals. After one frantic attack near the Oldham line Warrington were reduced to 11 men after prop Frank Shugars and centre Ike Taylor clashed heads and had to go off the pitch for treatment. Both returned, with bandaged heads, to savour the victory.

6 May 1950, Warrington 19–0 Widnes
Captain Harry Bath became the first overseas player to lift the Challenge Cup, which was presented by the Labour Prime Minister Clement Atlee. The Warrington players each received £40 winning pay and were allowed to keep their jerseys as souvenirs. Former captain Harold Palin kicked superbly, landing 4 goals and popping over a drop goal, but scrum-half Gerry Helme won the Lance Todd Trophy as man of the match.

5 May 1954, Warrington 8–4 Halifax
This Challenge Cup final replay at Odsal with an official attendance of 102,569 is one of the most famous games in the history of the sport because of that huge crowd. Tries from centre Jim Challinor and scrum-half Gerry Helme won the match and Warrington went on to complete the double for the only time in the club's history, beating the unfortunate Halifax side 8–7 in the Championship final at Maine Road.

11 May 1974, Warrington 24–9 Featherstone Rovers
This was all about player-coach and captain Alex Murphy, who had already led St Helens (1966) and Leigh (1971) to victory beneath the famous Twin Towers. Murphy himself contributed 2 drop goals while full-back Derek Whitehead won the Lance Todd Trophy after kicking 7 goals from all angles and distances. Hooker Kevin Ashcroft and second-row Mike Nicholas scored the tries. Nicholas, who had a fine game, suffered knee ligament damage in the second half which ruled him out of Great Britain's tour of Australia and New Zealand that summer and cost him the chance of a move to top Sydney club Manly.

29 August 2009, Warrington 25–16 Huddersfield
This final is best remembered for the exuberance of the 25,000 Warrington supporters in the new Wembley, although the players gave us plenty to cheer about. Full-back Richie Mathers scored the opening try after just 69 seconds and

the Wolves never looked back. Hooker Michael Monaghan, winger Chris Hicks and makeshift stand-off Vinnie Anderson also crossed. Centre Chris Bridge kicked 4 goals and scrum-half Lee Briers rounded things off nicely with a drop goal – his 60th for the club. Briers and captain Adrian Morley jointly collected the cup while Monaghan won the Lance Todd Trophy. What a day!

28 August 2010, Warrington 30–6 Leeds Rhinos
This final was supposed to be too close to call. Warrington coach Tony Smith even said that the Wolves were the underdogs, having lost twice to Leeds in the Super League that season. On the day, Warrington blew Leeds off the pitch with Australian wing Chris Hicks claiming the first hat-trick of tries at the new Wembley and centre Ryan Atkins crossing twice. Second-row Louis Anderson emulated his brother Vinnie from the previous year by scoring a try and Ben Westwood kicked 3 goals, but stand-off Lee Briers was a runaway winner of the Lance Todd Trophy after a near-perfect performance.

KICKING KINGS

One of the hallmarks of a great goal-kicker is to kick 100 goals in a season. It proves ability under pressure and consistency and only the best kickers achieve it.

Billy Holding (1928–40)
The Cumbrian full-back became the first Warrington player to kick 100 goals in a season in the 1930/31 campaign, but he only just made it, with 2 goals at Leigh on the last day taking him to 101. Two years later he extended his club record to 125 goals in a season as Warrington reached Wembley for the first time. Included in that total was possibly the greatest goal ever kicked by a Warrington player: at Central Park, Wigan,

in the third round of the Challenge Cup in March 1933. Wigan were leading 7–4 when Warrington scrum-half Dai Davies scored a try in the corner to level the scores with the conversion to come. After teeing-up the ball, Holding had to clear a path through the straw that had been used to protect the pitch and was stacked up around the touchline. Holding held his nerve and toe-poked the ball through the posts. Such was Holding's reputation that publicity posters in London ahead of the final invited supporters to, 'Come to Wembley to see Holding the wonder goal-kicker'. Holding kicked 100 goals in a season for the third and final time the following season. Holding also kicked more than 200 goals for the 'A' team, taking him well into four figures in the primrose and blue of Warrington. In Holding's day, rival full-backs would engage in kicking duels in open play to try to secure better field position for their side. Holding had many such duels with Swinton's Martin Hodgson, a fellow Cumbrian. Hodgson preferred a hard ball while Holding preferred one with a little softness about it. If Hodgson thought the ball was favouring Holding he would kick it over the stand in the hope that the replacement would be more to his liking. In one match, he did it three times until he got the ball he wanted.

Appearances: 328
Goals: 834
1930/31: 101 goals
1932/33: 125 goals
1933/34: 116 goals

Harold Palin (1936 and 1947/51)
Warrington-born Harold 'Moggy' Palin became the second Wire goal-kicker to kick 100 goals in a season and he did it in style, with a club record 146 during the 1948/49 campaign. Loose-forward Palin also became the first Warrington player to kick 10 goals in a match when he booted over 14 kicks during a Lancashire Cup tie against Liverpool Stanley at

Wilderspool in September 1950. Palin also kicked goals on the biggest stages, with three at Maine Road in May 1948 when Warrington beat Bradford Northern 15–5 in the Championship Final to be crowned rugby league champions for the first time. He also kicked 4 goals and a drop goal when Warrington thrashed Widnes 19–0 at Wembley in May 1950 to win the Challenge Cup.

Appearances: 150
Goals: 439 (including 3 drop goals)
1948/49: 146 goals
1949/50: 133 goals

Harry Bath (1948–57)
Harold Palin's club record of 146 goals in a season did not last long because the great Harry Bath eclipsed it in the 1952/53 campaign when he was successful with 162 shots at goal. That season was the start of a golden period for the Australian forward who kicked 100 goals in four consecutive seasons. Like Palin, he kicked 10 goals in a match (three times) and kicked goals on the biggest stages. In the all-conquering 1953/54 season, when Warrington completed the league and cup double for the only time in the club's history, he was on target in all the important games – at Wembley, at Odsal and at Maine Road. As well as being a champion goal-kicker, Bath also scored 90 tries in the primrose and blue of Warrington – including one at Wembley in 1950 when he became the first overseas player to lift the Challenge Cup as captain. Bath returned home to Australia in 1957 and kicked 108 goals for Sydney St George in the 1958 season.

Appearances: 346
Goals: 812
1952/53: 162 goals
1953/54: 153 goals
1954/55: 118 goals
1955/56: 154 goals

Eric Fraser (1951–64)

Eric Fraser kicked 100 goals in a season in the 1960/61 campaign to help Warrington finish second in the league and qualify for their ninth and last Championship Final, against Leeds at Odsal where the Wire lost 25–10 to a Lewis Jones-inspired side. However, the most important goal he kicked for the club had come the previous season when he converted Brian Bevan's try against St Helens in the Lancashire Cup final at Central Park, from near the touchline and in front of 39,237 supporters, to give Warrington the trophy. Fraser, probably the greatest full-back in the club's history, never kicked 10 goals in a match for Warrington but did achieve the feat twice, once for Great Britain against North Queensland when he landed 15 goals and once for Lancashire against Cumberland when he kicked 12. Both games were in 1958.

Appearances: 352
Goals: 473
1960/61: 103 goals

Keith Affleck (1963–9)

After joining the Wire from the local amateur side Rylands, full-back Keith Affleck became only the fifth Warrington player to kick 100 goals in a season during the 1966/67 campaign. He reached the landmark during the last league game, against Swinton at Wilderspool. The following season he kicked 9 goals in a match against Doncaster.

Appearances: 88 + 8 as a substitute
Goals: 199 (including 2 drop goals)
1966/67: 102 goals

Jeff Bootle (1964–9)

Full-back Jeff Bootle kicked two goals in the 1965 Lancashire Cup final when he captained the Wire to a 16–5 victory over Rochdale Hornets at Knowsley Road, but it was another

3 years before he kicked 100 goals in a season. It was well worth the wait, however, as he finished the 1968/69 campaign with 125 goals, including 3 drop goals, and 7 tries for an impressive haul of 271 points.

Appearances: 165 + 6 as a substitute
Goals: 345
1968/69: 125 goals

Derek Whitehead (1969–79)

Stand by for a terrible pun. Full-back Derek Whitehead, a butcher by trade, joined Warrington from Oldham in September 1969 and soon proved to be a cut above his new team-mates in the goal-kicking department. Well, I did warn you. In fact, he quickly established himself as one of the best goal-kickers in the club's history. Whitehead was one of the last front-on, toe-pokers and kicked 100 goals in three successive seasons from 1971/72. Each season was better than the last until in 1973/74 he equalled Harry Bath's club record with 162 shots on target, including 7 drop goals. Warrington won four cups that season and Whitehead kicked goals in all four finals, including 7 at Wembley to earn the Lance Todd Trophy as man of the match. When Whitehead was inducted into the club's Hall of Fame in 2008 he was asked if he had tried the more modern, round-the-corner kicking style used today. Whitehead admitted that he had, but the ball had disappeared in every direction except the one intended. He had decided to stick with what he knew best, with excellent results.

Appearances: 245 + 29 as a substitute
Goals: 734 (including 21 drop goals)
1971/72: 106 goals
1972/73: 136 goals
1973/74: 162 goals

THE WARRINGTON WOLVES MISCELLANY   117

Steve Hesford (1975–85)

Steve Hesford wanted to be a goalkeeper just like his dad, Bob, who had played for Huddersfield Town in the 1938 FA Cup final and even followed his dream to Wollongong in Australia. After 18 months he returned home disillusioned and began playing rugby union for Fleetwood. That's how desperate he had become. But there he was spotted by Albert White, the Warrington scout, and offered trials at Wilderspool. The rest, as they say, is history as Steve 'The Boot' kicked his way into the record books. He kicked 100 goals in a season for 8 consecutive seasons and, during the 1978/79 campaign, he popped over 170 kicks for a club record that still stands. His career goals total and points total both set records, although Lee Briers snatched the latter in May 2011. Amazingly, Hesford never kicked 10 goals in a match but by just about every other criteria he was the best the club has known. Another miscellaneous fact about Hesford is that he was born in Zambia. Not many people know that. Hesford's brilliant goal-kicking caught up with him in 1993 when he had to have a hip replacement.

Appearances: 310 + 8 as a substitute
Goals: 1,159 (including 47 drop goals)
1976/77: 129 goals
1977/78: 158 goals
1978/79: 170 goals
1979/80: 128 goals
1980/81: 147 goals
1981/82: 116 goals
1982/83: 113 goals
1983/84: 142 goals

Paul Bishop (1984–90)

Left-footed Paul Bishop is best remembered for kicking drop goals and kicked 17 of them – a club record for one season – on his way to kicking 100 goals during the 1986/87 campaign. The previous season he had become the first Warrington player to kick 5 drop goals in a match – at Wigan in the Premiership semi-final. Each one was like a stake into the Wigan heart as Warrington won 23–12. Bishop also kicked goals on the biggest stage of all, Wembley, with 2 in the 1990 Challenge Cup final.

Appearances: 102 + 11 as a substitute
Goals: 225 (including 42 drop goals)
1986/87: 116 goals

John Woods (1987–9)
John Woods only spent two seasons at Wilderspool but kicked 100 goals each time. His first season, 1987/88, was quite extraordinary as he kicked 152 goals – making him the leading goal-kicker in the country – and scored 13 tries to finish up with a grand total of 351 points. His second season was almost as good before, in July 1989, he was sold to Rochdale Hornets for £50,000. Woods was, without doubt, the best player never to play at Wembley. Not many rugby league players can be described as graceful, but John could.

Appearances: 72
Goals: 259 (including 5 drop goals)
1987/88: 152 goals
1988/89: 107 goals

Jonathan Davies (1993–5)
Like John Woods, Jonathan Davies only spent two full seasons at Wilderspool, but kicked 100 goals each time – and made it look easy. For good measure, in his first season, he was also Warrington's leading try-scorer. When rugby union finally went professional in 1995 Davies was the first player they took back when he left Warrington for Cardiff on 31 October in a reported £100,000 transfer deal.

Appearances: 66
Goals: 258 (including 26 drop goals)
1993/94: 110 goals
1994/95: 116 goals

Lee Briers (1997–)
As befits a player who wears his heart on his sleeve, Lee Briers is a confidence kicker. When he is playing well and feeling good, he can kick goals from anywhere and make it look easy. One of his good days came against York at Wilderspool in the Challenge Cup in February 2000 when he kicked 14 goals to equal Harold Palin's club record. He also kicked the first goal at The Halliwell Jones Stadium in February 2004 when he converted Nathan Wood's try. Finally, after a number of near misses, he kicked 100 in a season in 2006 to join this elite group. Also that year he broke Steve Hesford's career drop goal record with his 1-pointer at Bradford in April. The 2011 season was another memorable one with Briers thriving in the role of understudy to Brett Hodgson. He kicked 12 goals against Keighley in the fourth round of the Challenge Cup and topped that with a record-breaking 16 against Swinton in the next round. Briers has also embraced and mastered a kicking skill that was not needed by any of his illustrious predecessors – the 40/20 kick, which was introduced in 1999.

Appearances: 366 + 13 as a substitute
Goals: 979 (including a club record 68 drop goals)
2006: 123 goals

Brett Hodgson (2011–)
Eyebrows were raised when Tony Smith replaced Richie Mathers (26) with Brett Hodgson (32) but supporters had no need to worry. As well as signing an outstanding full-back, Smith had also recruited a wonderful goal-kicker who reached his century of goals in just 19 games and with an 80 per cent success rate. Along the way, he kicked 13 against Harlequins

and 10 each against Crusaders and Salford. Hodgson was born in Liverpool. Liverpool, New South Wales that is. In 2011, Hodgson scored 18 tries for a total of 318 points, the best seasonal tally of his career.

Appearances: 27
Goals: 123

DERBY DAYS: WIRE V CHEMICS

In recent years, Warrington's derbies against Wigan and St Helens have meant more to all concerned, but for many years it was Warrington against Widnes, the Wire against the Chemics, that set pulses racing. The intense rivalry can be traced all the way back to the first meeting at Warrington on 19 January 1878. Newspaper reports said the visit of Widnes produced a match with 'some fierceness on both sides'. Spectators at Arpley spilled on to the pitch and 'a boy in the crowd was struck by the ball, and had a narrow escape of tumbling into the Mersey.'

Warrington's first 10,000 crowd was also for the visit of Widnes in the second round of the West Lancashire and Border Towns Cup in March 1886. About 2,000 fans made the journey from Widnes on special trains. In truth, the crowd was probably too big for the Wilderspool Road ground and, early in the second half, play was suddenly suspended by the collapse of the grandstand which contained about 200 people. No one was seriously hurt, although a few people received bruises and were slightly shaken.

Fast forward to last century and the two rivals clashed in two Challenge Cup finals at Wembley, with Warrington winning 19–0 in 1950 and Widnes taking their revenge with a 14–7 victory in 1975. They also met in two John Player Trophy finals (1978 and 1979) with Warrington again winning the first but losing the second.

Games between the two clubs in the 1970s featured running battles between two Welshmen, Big Jim Mills of Widnes and Warrington's 'Clunk Click Mike Nick' (Mike Nicholas). Those two characters were replaced by two overseas players in the 1980s, King Kurt Sorensen of Widnes and New Zealand and Sir Les Boyd of Warrington and Australia.

In 2003, taking the rivalry into a third century, Widnes kicked up a stink about a promotional poster which depicted the town as an industrial wasteland while, on Good Friday 2004, the Vikings became the first visiting team to win at The Halliwell Jones Stadium. In 2005, Warrington won 60–16 at Widnes to condemn them to relegation.

It almost goes without saying but the leading try-scorer in these derby fixtures was Brian Bevan who ran in 31 tries in 32 appearances.

PLAYER OF THE 1990S – MARK FORSTER (1983–2000)

Any boy who grew up in the 1960s will be able to tell you that the Gerry Anderson character Captain Scarlet was indestructible. The same seems to be true of the Warrington winger Mark Forster. He started playing for Warrington's 'A' team at Wilderspool on Friday nights while he was still a pupil at Richard Fairclough High School and turning out for Woolston Rovers. Twenty years later, he was still playing for Warrington's first team and preparing for his second testimonial season. After that, he played for Widnes. And after that he played for Rylands Sharks when he was well into his forties. And, for more than two decades, in good teams and in not-so-good teams, he averaged a try every other game. Like all top-quality wingers, he was fast. He proved just how fast in November 1986 when he beat all his rivals in the Whitbread Trophy Bitter Sprint before the third Test between Great Britain and Australia at Wigan. Forster's prize was a cheque for £1,000 and the knowledge that he was the fastest man in the British game. Forster lost that particular crown when Widnes signed the freakishly quick Martin Offiah, but he remained the fastest man at Wilderspool, with the possible exception of Des Drummond, until well past his 30th birthday. By then he was claiming to be the strongest man at the club and at 5ft 10in and 15 stones not many were prepared to argue with him.

Increasingly, Forster used his strength to support his forwards and his huge appetite for work was one of the reasons he was named the *Warrington Guardian* Sports Personality of the Year in 1997. Primarily, however, he is remembered as a prolific try-scorer and his tally of 191 puts him comfortably in fourth place in the club's all-time list behind Brian Bevan (740), Jack Fish (214) and John Bevan (201). He also had the knack of scoring important tries, including 6 in major finals. His most important try, however, was probably the one against Oldham in the 1990 Challenge Cup semi-final at Central Park, which sealed Warrington's return to Wembley after a gap of 15 years. Forster latched on to a pass from substitute Mark Thomas and touched down in the corner for a regulation winger's try.

He scored tries against every other Super League club, including 17 against Wigan and 15 against St Helens. He also made a point of scoring against Wigan in the annual pre-season Locker Cup games, including a hat-trick in the 1989 match. Fittingly, he marked his 400th appearance for the club, against Bradford Bulls at Wilderspool in June 1998, with a man-of-the-match performance and two tries in a 21–10 victory. In representative games, he played for Lancashire, Great Britain Under-21s, Great Britain and, finally, Ireland, courtesy of an Irish grandmother, in the 2000 Rugby League World Cup. Then he joined Widnes in the Northern Ford Premiership and scored his 200th career try before joining Rylands Sharks. And finally, in the 2010/11 season, he played for Bank Quay

Bulls, with both his sons, Danny and Chris, in the same team. Indestructible indeed.

Appearances: 442 + 16 as a substitute
Tries: 191
Goals: 3
Points: 769

Honours: Premiership Trophy 1985/86
Lancashire Cup 1989/90
Regal Trophy: 1990/91

30 POINTS IN A MATCH

In a team sport like rugby league nobody wins a match on their own, although if you score 30 points or more in the 80 minutes, like the following players have, it must feel like it.

44 (3T & 16G)	Lee Briers v Swinton	H	20 May 201	Chall Cup
40 (3T & 14G)	Lee Briers v York	H	27 Feb 2000	Chall Cup
34 (4T & 9G)	Graham Appo v Halifax	H	27 July 2003	SL
32 (2T & 12G)	Lee Briers v Keighley	H	7 May 2011	Chall Cup
32 (3T & 10G)	Graham Appo v Wakefield	H	21 Sept 2003	SL
31 (5T & 8G)	George Thomas v St Helens	H	12 April 1909	Lge
30 (4T & 9G)	Jack Fish v Huddersfield	H	20 Oct 1906	Lge
30 (3T & 9G)	Chris Hicks v Bradford	A	17 April 2009	SL
30 (1T & 13G)	Brett Hodgson v Harlequins	H	20 March 2011	SL

STRIKE RATE

The try-scorers with the best strike rates are as follows:

1 Brian Bevan (740 in 620 apps) 1.19 tries per game
2 Joel Monaghan (30 in 26) 1.15 tries per game
3 Bobby Fulton (16 in 16) 1 try per game
4 Phil Blake (41 in 44) 0.93 tries per game
5 Chris Hicks (71 in 82) 0.86 tries per game
6 Izzy Davies (57 in 69) 0.83 tries per game
7 Henry Fa'afili (73 in 97) 0.75 tries per game
8 Richie Myler (38 in 51) 0.74 tries per game
9 Nigel Vagana (22 in 30) 0.73 tries per game

Players must have played 15 games to qualify.

FINEST FRONT ROWS

Every generation will have their particular favourite but the all-British combination of Chisnall, Ashcroft and Brady was a big hit in the early 1970s. Prop Dave Chisnall and hooker Kevin Ashcroft both played for Great Britain while Brian Brady played for Lancashire and is the club's record try-scoring prop, with 50 of his 54 tries coming from that position.

The mid-1980s brought the all-Antipodean grouping of Boyd, Tamati and Jackson, with the two Aussie props, Sir Les Boyd and Bob Jackson, packing down around Kiwi hooker Kevin Tamati. All three were hard men but all three served as team captain at one time or another. Present-day fans, meanwhile, will point to Morley, Monaghan and Carvell as a fearsome unit, with the British beef of Adrian Morley and Garreth Carvell complementing the play-making skills of the Australian Michael Monaghan.

BEATING THE AUSSIES

Believe it or not, Warrington have a better record against Australia than either England or Great Britain, having won 8 and drawn 1 of their 16 meetings with the Kangaroos. It helped, of course, that all 16 meetings were at Wilderspool but every victory was special.

14 November 1908, Warrington 10–3 Australia
Tries from winger Jack Fish and centre Ike Taylor put Warrington in command. On the stroke of full time, captain George Dickenson kicked a drop goal – the ball dropped on the crossbar and bounced over – to seal the victory. This was the first match for which programmes were on sale, priced 1*d*, though worth considerably more now.

29 October 1921, Warrington 8–5 Australia
Ten teams had already tried and failed to beat the Kangaroos before they arrived at Wilderspool. Full-back Ben Jolley was the Wire hero with 4 penalty goals. The match attracted a crowd of 16,000 – who paid ground record receipts of £1,700. During the latter stages, however, the gates were thrown open and at least 2,000 more supporters packed in to see a thrilling victory.

21 December 1929, Warrington 17–8 Australia
The winger who would become known as Tommy 'Tubby' Thompson was only a slip of a lad at the time, aged 20, but still scored all the points – 3 tries and 4 goals – as Warrington recorded a famous victory. Amazingly, Warrington had four players away on County Championship duty and an unknown rugby union trialist at stand-off.

14 October 1933, Warrington 15–12 Australia
Australia had forward Ray Stehr, a Sydney policeman back home, sent off for foul play just before half time to make things a little easier. Welsh forward Arthur 'Candy' Evans

scored 2 tries while Bill Shankland, the Warrington captain, produced an excellent display against his fellow countryman. After the match, the Kangaroos needed three cabin trunks to carry away all the presents – seven for each member of the tour party – they had been given by the club and local businesses.

27 November 1937, Warrington 8–6 Australia
Australia were accused of 'vigorous and shady tactics' by the press and had another forward, Gordon MacLennan, sent off 15 minutes from time. Warrington scrum-half Frank Cueto levelled the scores at 6–6 with a brilliant solo try before Bill Shankland kicked the winning penalty goal.

30 October 1948, Warrington 16–7 Australia
A crowd of 26,879 turned up to watch this one and were rewarded with 5 goals from captain and loose-forward Harold Palin. Scrum-half Gerry Helme and second-row Jim Featherstone scored the tries as Warrington, the champions of England, won comfortably.

27 October 1956, Warrington 21–17 Australia
Two tries apiece from centre Jim Challinor and his winger Laurie Gilfedder helped the Wire to win a thrilling contest. Australian forward Harry Bath showed his homeland what they were missing with 3 goals. Another Australian, winger Len Horton, scored the 5th Warrington try.

11 October 1978, Warrington 15–12 Australia
This was one of Wilderspool's most famous nights because the odds were stacked impossibly high against Warrington. Stand-off Ken Kelly had been ordered to play for Lancashire against Cumbria in Whitehaven on the same night and the club had been told to rest Great Britain winger John Bevan ahead of the Wales v Australia match at Swansea 4 days later. Also, scrum-half Parry Gordon was injured, but the players remaining rose to the challenge magnificently. Seventeen

minutes from time, with Warrington trailing 12–10, Australia had full-back Allan McMahon sent off for biting player-coach Billy Benyon. Ten minutes from time stand-in stand-off Ronnie Clark made a break, stand-in scrum-half Alan Gwilliam took over, kicked ahead and won the race for the touchdown, despite Australian protests that he had not grounded the ball properly. Hesford's conversion – his 6th goal of the night – sealed the victory. The Kangaroos hated it, refusing to shake hands at the final whistle and leaving Wilderspool in double-quick time.

Warrington: Finnigan; M. Kelly, Hesford, Benyon, Walsh; Clark, Gwilliam; Lester, Cunningham, Nicholas, Martyn, Case, Potter. Subs: Hunter, Whittaker.

Wilderspool only staged one Anglo-Australian Test match, the third and deciding Test between Great Britain and Australia on 1 December 1973 and again a Warrington-born player took centre stage. Sadly, on this occasion, it was stand-off Bobby Fulton, whose family had emigrated when he was a toddler and who scored their first try in a 15–5 victory.

PLAYER OF THE 'NOUGHTIES' – LEE BRIERS (1997–)

The venue was The Halliwell Jones Stadium and the Sky TV cameras were in town for a live broadcast. Lee Briers scored a try near the posts and no Warrington supporter needs to be reminded what happened next. He sat down in the stand to reflect on his good work. It was great television and a wonderful insight into the thinking of one of the club's all-time most popular players. Talented? Yes. Loyal? Yes. A match-winner? Of course. But also a man of the people, one of the boys, a cheeky chappie and a mischief-maker all rolled into one. In other words, a typical top-quality half-back.

Warrington coach Darryl Van de Velde made Briers his first signing, from St Helens, in April 1997 for a reported £65,000. Briers was still only 18 and has repaid that modest investment many times over as he has carved his name into the club's history. In February 2000, he smashed a long-standing club record by scoring 40 points in a match (3 tries and 14 goals) in a Challenge Cup tie against York. The following year he produced one of the great performances in a beaten Warrington side when he scored 3 tries and kicked 3 goals in a Challenge Cup semi-final against Bradford.

That display caught the eye of the Welsh Rugby Union but he rejected their overtures as he would later turn down offers to join Widnes and Barrow. His loyalty was rewarded with the club captaincy from 2002 to 2007, a testimonial season and, best of all, key roles in the back-to-back Challenge Cup final wins of 2009 and 2010. Against Huddersfield in the 2009 final, he calmed nerves with a late drop goal, his 60th for the club, before he jointly collected the cup with new captain Adrian Morley. In 2010, he went one better, with a masterful display against Leeds Rhinos to win the Lance Todd Trophy as man of the match.

Briers broke down in tears after the 2009 semi-final victory over Wigan, coming as it did, on the eighth anniversary of his brother Brian's death from cancer. Brian would have been 43 that very day. Perhaps that real personal tragedy helped him to come to terms with a series of Great Britain coaches failing to recognise his talents, despite a vocal 'Briers for Britain' campaign, although he did earn one cap against France in 2001. Wales (which he has also captained) and Warrington have reaped the benefit of those talents and continue to do so. Briers added three more records to his collection in 2011: most goals in a match (16, against Swinton), most points in a match (44, against Swinton) and most points in a career (breaking Steve Hesford's 26-year-old mark).

Appearances: 366 + 13 as a substitute
Tries: 144
Goals: 911
Drop goals: 68
Points: 2,466
Honours: Challenge Cup 2009 and 2010.

SHORT BUT SWEET

Some players have made a lasting impression at the club despite only having a relatively short career in primrose and blue, including the following:

Andrew Johns (2005): Yes, Joey was a Wire. It was only for 3 games – and he reportedly picked up £10,000 per match – but it was fun while it lasted. His debut against Leeds at The Halliwell Jones Stadium was the stuff of fairytales. Johns kicked off, Rob Burrow was trampled underfoot by Chris Leikvoll, Warrington won the scrum and Henry Fa'afili scored in the corner after 52 seconds. Six Johns goals and a Johns drop goal later and Warrington had beaten the reigning Super League champions 33–16. The Wolves won at Hull 6 days later before the black and whites gained their revenge in the play-off game at The Halliwell Jones Stadium. Johns has made a couple of trips back to Warrington since to help with pre-season training.

Bobby Fulton (1969–70): Sixteen appearances for a pretty ordinary Warrington side brought Fulton 16 tries and his half-back partnership with Parry Gordon still ranks as one of the best in the club's history. Fulton was an Aussie, and a World Cup-winning Aussie at that, but he had been born in Stockton Heath before his family emigrated when he was a toddler so that made it even better. Fulton made one more appearance at Wilderspool in December 1973, scoring the opening try as Australia beat Great Britain 15–5 in the third and deciding Ashes Test.

Dave Wright (1973–4): Wright was a second-row forward who played 25 games during the all-conquering 1973/74 season and Warrington won 22 of them, including the Captain Morgan Trophy final, the Player's No. 6 Trophy final and the Challenge Cup final at Wembley, which was his last appearance for the club. After that he returned home to Australia, exhausted but happy, and was capped by the Kangaroos in 1975. He has made a couple of visits back to Warrington, including in 1999, when the Wembley winners of 1974 all got together for the last time to mark the silver anniversary of their triumph under the Twin Towers.

Allan Langer (2000/01): Tempting Alfie out of retirement was Darryl Van de Velde's greatest triumph and the 5ft 5in scrum-half even rebuffed a late bid from Wigan to come to Wilderspool. His Wolves career lasted just 18 months (55 appearances) and was a joy to watch. One of my favourite moments came against St Helens at Wilderspool in April 2000. Langer sent a grubber kick into the St Helens in-goal area and Tommy Martyn (no mean player himself) collected it. But before Martyn knew what had happened, Langer had grabbed the ball out of his hands and touched down for a try. Priceless. Langer also made a man-of-the-match performance for Queensland against New South Wales in the deciding State of Origin game in Brisbane in July 2001.

Kevin Penny (2006–9): When Kevin Penny burst on to the scene, aged 19, with 13 tries in 13 appearances at the end of the 2007 season, it wasn't just Warrington fans who thought they had seen a star in the making. Penny's dazzling wing play earned him a place in that year's Super League Dream Team and a call-up to the Great Britain squad. Penny scored a hat-trick in 8 minutes against Salford at The Halliwell Jones

Stadium when the third was a length-of-the field sprint to reach Lee Briers' kick. He scored another wonder try at St Helens, in front of the TV cameras, in the Challenge Cup in 2008 but that was followed by a blunder which set Saints on their way to victory. His star faded after that with spells on loan to Widnes (2009) and Harlequins (2010) before a transfer to Wakefield, aged just 23.

Joe Hartley (1905): Signed from Bradford Northern, this 6ft 2in and 13st 12lb Cumberland county forward only made one appearance. It was at Widnes in December 1905 and he was sent off for fighting and banned for three weeks. That's consistency for you!

LEADING TRY-SCORERS FOR EVERY POSITION

Full-back	Lee Penny	91
Right wing	Brian Bevan	738
Right centre	Jim Challinor	109
Left centre	Billy Dingsdale	129
Left wing	John Bevan	122
Stand-off	Bobby Greenough	92
Scrum-half	Parry Gordon	164
Prop	Brian Brady	50
Hooker	Harold 'Ike' Fishwick	32
Second-row	Harry Bath	82
Loose-forward	Charlie Seeling	37
Substitute	Paul Wood	21

(to end of 2011 season)

All also scored tries from other positions. Bob Eccles is the club's all-time highest scoring forward, with 118 of his 119 tries coming from positions in the pack. He also scored 1 try as a centre at Hull KR in September 1985.

COACHES

Ces Mountford (1951–61)
Played: 433
Won: 282   65 per cent
Drew: 13   3 per cent
Lost: 138   32 per cent
First game: Huddersfield away on 18 August 1951.
  Warrington won 13-9.
Last game: v Leeds at Odsal in the Championship final on 20
  May 1961. Warrington lost 25–10 in front of a crowd of
  52,177.
Honours: Championship 1953/54 and 1954/55
Challenge Cup 1953/54
Lancashire Cup 1959/60
Television Trophy 1955/56
Lancashire League 1953/54, 1954/55 and 1955/56

Verdict: Simply the best. The brains behind Warrington's
greatest team, he arrived at Wilderspool from Wigan on an
unprecedented 10-year contract in the summer of 1951 and
only left in 1961 when the board would only offer him a
contract for a further 5 years. Mountford said he would not
accept a deal for less than 7 years. He was passionate about
his job and in March 1959 he was ordered by the RFL to
apologise in writing to referee Eric Clay for remarks made
after Warrington had lost 13-3 at Leigh in the second round of
the Challenge Cup. He was much loved by his former players,
two of whom visited him at his home in New Zealand to find
that his house was called 'Central Park'. Nobody's perfect.
He died in 2009, aged 90, a giant of the sport.

Ernie Ashcroft (1961–7)
Played: 252
Won: 133   53 per cent
Drew: 9   4 per cent
Lost: 110   44 per cent
First game: Hull away on 19 August 1961. Warrington won 16–14.
Last game: Bradford away in the first round of the Championship play-offs on 15 April 1967. Warrington lost 12–6.
Honours: Lancashire Cup 1965/66
Wigan Sevens 1965/66

Verdict: Like Mountford, Ashcroft had been a great player at Wigan before taking charge at Wilderspool. He had also coached Huddersfield, but, at Warrington, he was taking over a team which was in decline. He resigned in May 1967 after becoming disillusioned with the role.

Jackie Fleming (1967–8)
Played: 67
Won: 41   61 per cent
Drew: 1   1 per cent
Lost: 25   37 per cent
First game: v Blackpool Borough at home in the first round of the Lancashire Cup on 19 August 1967. Warrington won 17–10.
Last game: v Leeds at home on 18 December 1968. Warrington lost 16–9.
Honours: Lancashire League 1967/68

Verdict: Fleming had been a great player for Warrington and was the stand-off when the Wire were crowned champions for the first time by beating Bradford Northern 15–5 in the 1948 Championship Final. As a coach, he over-achieved in his first season, guiding Warrington to the Lancashire League title with a 7–6 victory at Leigh on the last day of the regular season. He paid the price for that the following season. Warrington's 29–6 defeat at St Helens in the semi-finals of the BBC2 Floodlit Trophy cost him his job. He was not sacked until after the next game, at home to Leeds, although the decision had already been taken before kick-off. Fleming was told he was not getting the best out of the squad and that there was 'friction' in the camp after he had disciplined players for missing training.

Joe Egan (1968–70)
Played: 73
Won: 32   44 per cent
Drew: 4   5 per cent
Lost: 37   51 per cent
First game: Wigan away on 1 January 1969. Warrington won 23–18.
Last game: Featherstone away on 17 October 1970. Warrington lost 21–16.

Verdict: Egan had already coached Leigh, Wigan and Widnes and so knew the drill and his reign got off to the perfect start with the 23–18 win at Central Park on New Year's Day 1969. Wigan had been unbeaten in their previous 14 matches. Warrington, however, were starting to suffer from financial problems and a few weeks later were forced to sell prop Keith Ashcroft to Wigan for £3,000. As results started to suffer, Egan eventually resigned in September 1970. A former Great Britain hooker, Egan was still going strong, aged 90, in 2009 and was featured in the Warrington v Huddersfield Challenge Cup final programme under the clever headline 'Joe 90'.

Peter Harvey (1970–1)
Played: 26
Won: 12   46 per cent
Drew: 1   4 per cent
Lost: 13   50 per cent
First game: Hull KR home on 23 October 1970. Warrington
    won 15–10.
Last game: Huyton away on 18 April 1971. Warrington won
    16–9.

Verdict: Peter Harvey never stood a chance. Promoted from being 'A' team coach after Joe Egan resigned, the odds were always stacked against him as chairman Walter Challinor announced that unless £10,000 was raised before the end of the season the club would close. Harvey struggled to raise two teams every weekend and even had to worry about the posts falling down because the wood was starting to go rotten.

Alex Murphy (1971–8)
Played: 308
Won: 176   57 per cent
Drew: 14   5 per cent
Lost: 118   38 per cent
First game: Whitehaven home in the first round of the
    Lancashire Cup on 6 August 1971. Warrington won 17–9
    with Murphy scoring a try and kicking a goal and a drop
    goal.
Last game: Widnes away in the first round of the Premiership
    on 29 April 1978. Warrington lost 33–8.
Honours: League Leaders' Shield 1972/73
Challenge Cup 1973/74
Player's No. 6/John Player Trophy 1973/74 and 1977/78
Captain Morgan Trophy 1973/74
Club Championship 1973/74

Verdict: A golden age for the club when there was never a dull moment. Winning the Challenge Cup at Wembley in 1974, 20 years after the club's last success in the competition, was extra special, as was lifting four cups that season. Murphy, in effect, built two teams, the Wembley winners of Kevin Ashcroft, Dave Chisnall, Dave Wright and John Bevan and the 1978 John Player Trophy team of Steve Hesford, Ken Kelly, Tommy Martyn and Ian Potter.

Billy Benyon (1978–82)
Played: 154
Won: 93   60 per cent
Drew: 6   4 per cent
Lost: 55   36 per cent
First game: Swinton home in the first round of the Lancashire Cup on 20 August 1978. Warrington won 18–4.
Last game: Hull KR away on 3 March 1982. Warrington lost 16–10.
Honours: Lancashire Cup 1980/81
John Player Trophy 1980/81.

Verdict: Benyon was coach of the year for the 1980/81 season after Warrington won the Lancashire Cup and John Player Trophy and just missed out on the First Division title. He was also the player coach when Warrington beat Australia 15–12 on an unforgettable Wilderspool night in October 1978. He deserved better treatment than being sacked in March 1982 – a fact borne out when he won his case for unfair dismissal at an industrial tribunal in September 1982. In January 1983, he was awarded £3,968 in compensation.

Kevin Ashcroft (1982–4)
Played: 90
Won: 50   56 per cent
Drew: 5   6 per cent
Lost: 35   39 per cent

First game: Hull KR home on 7 March 1982. Warrington
   won 14–6.
Last game: St Helens home in the first round of the
   Premiership on 29 April 1984. Warrington lost 19–13.
Honours: Lancashire Cup 1982/83.

Verdict: Ashcroft was a popular coach who maintained
Warrington's position as one of the leading clubs. Third place
in the First Division at the end of the 1983/84 season was a
fine achievement.

Reg Bowden (1984–6)
Played: 61
Won: 32   52 per cent
Drew: 0   0 per cent
Lost: 29   48 per cent
First game: Widnes home on 2 September 1984. Warrington
   lost 20–18.
Last game: Oldham away in the second round of the
   Challenge Cup on 9 March 1986. Warrington lost 13–6.

Verdict: Bowden had been a great scrum-half at Widnes and
a fine player-coach at Fulham, but could not repeat those
successes at Warrington.

Tony Barrow (1986–8)
Played: 109
Won: 68   62 per cent
Drew: 4   4 per cent
Lost: 37   34 per cent
First game: Salford away on 16 March 1986. Warrington
   won 19–10.
Last game: Oldham home in the first round of the John
   Player Special Trophy on 13 November 1988. Warrington
   won 21–14.
Honours: Premiership Trophy 1985/86, **British Coal Nines**
   1988

Verdict: Barrow was a top-class, modern-style coach whose team was respected throughout the game – even by Wigan who were just starting to monopolise all the major trophies. Barrow only resigned because he thought the board wanted to replace him with an Australian coach.

Brian Johnson (1988–96)
Played: 260
Won: 140   54 per cent
Drew: 8   3 per cent
Lost: 112   43 per cent
First game: Bramley home in the second round of the John Player Special Trophy on 27 November 1988. Warrington won 42–10.
Last game: St Helens away in the Regal Trophy semi-final on 4 January 1996. Warrington suffered a club record 80–0 defeat.
Honours: Regal Trophy 1990/91
Lancashire Cup 1989/90

Verdict: Highly-respected and deep-thinking Australian coach who got the best out of the players in his squad. The 1993/94 season, when Warrington missed out on the First Division title on points difference, was one of many highlights, as was Wembley 1990. He deserved a better fate than to suffer a club record defeat in his last game in charge.

John Dorahy (1996–7)
Played: 30
Won: 15   50 per cent
Drew: 0   0 per cent
Lost: 15   50 per cent
First game: Oldham away in the fourth round of the Challenge Cup on 4 February 1996. Warrington won 26–4.
Last game: Sheffield away in Super League on 28 March 1997. Warrington lost 32–18.

Verdict: Dorahy had won the league and cup double with Wigan in 1993/94 but growing financial pressures meant that he quickly ran out of time at Warrington. Signing centre Nigel Vagana from Auckland Warriors, though, was a masterstroke.

Darryl Van de Velde (1997–2001)
Played: 140
Won: 59   42 per cent
Drew: 3   2 per cent
Lost: 78   56 per cent
First game: Oldham home on 6 April 1997. Warrington won 28–18.
Last game: Wakefield away on 29 July 2001. Warrington won 19–18.

Verdict: DVDV's reign was a rollercoaster ride of breathtaking highs and bewildering lows. His first move was to sign half-back Lee Briers, 18, from St Helens for a reported £65,000 and he has become one of the club's playing legends. He also led Warrington to Challenge Cup semi-finals in 2000 and 2001, both against a fearsome Bradford Bulls side, but both ended in defeat. Signing Allan Langer and making him captain was another inspired move but DVDV's side lost more matches than it won.

Steve Anderson (2001–2)
Played: 14
Won: 4   29 per cent
Drew: 1   7 per cent
Lost: 9   64 per cent
First game: Castleford home on 12 August 2001. Warrington won 27–12.
Last game: Wakefield away on 7 April 2002. Warrington lost 32–20 to go bottom of the Super League.

Verdict: Widnes coach Neil Kelly was the first choice for the job but changed his mind after the Vikings won promotion to Super League. Anderson was in charge for less than a year and only two incidents stick out from that grim time. The first was the club record 84–12 defeat at home to Bradford in September 2001. The second was the front page comment article in the *Warrington Guardian* in April 2002 headlined 'Kick Ando Into Touch' and featuring a picture of his face superimposed on a rugby ball. Dark days indeed.

David Plange (2002)
Played: 16
Won: 4   25 per cent
Drew: 0   0 per cent
Lost: 12   75 per cent
First game: Wigan away on 19 April 2002. Warrington lost 58–4.
Last game: Castleford home on 11 August 2002. Warrington lost 24–12.

Verdict: Plange arrived at Wilderspool as Anderson's assistant and was left with a near-impossible job when he left. He did make three key signings – Graham Appo, Nathan Wood and Ben Westwood – but they arrived too late to save him. The 72–2 defeat at St Helens in August was humiliating and helped make Plange, statistically at least, the least successful coach in the club's history.

Paul Cullen (2002–8)
Played: 179
Won: 87   49 per cent
Drew: 2   1 per cent
Lost: 90   50 per cent
First game: Widnes away on 18 August 2002. Warrington lost 19–18.
Last game: Castleford home on 26 May 2008. Warrington lost 36–28 after leading 28–14 with 10 minutes left.

Verdict: Paul Cullen laid the foundations for the success the Wolves enjoy today. He saved the club from relegation in 2002 and then led the team into the play-offs for the first time the following season to provide Wilderspool with a fitting send-off. Under his common-sense coaching, Warrington closed the gap on the Big Four until the Wolves were regularly beating three of them – Wigan, Leeds and Bradford. Only St Helens remained tantalisingly out of reach. After St Helens had won 30–22 at The Halliwell Jones Stadium in April 2008, Saints coach Daniel Anderson admitted, 'Warrington were very, very good – we were just a little bit better.' Cullen also appointed Adrian Morley as captain.

James Lowes (2008–9)
Played: 16
Won: 7   44 per cent
Drew: 0   0 per cent
Lost: 9   56 per cent
First game: Harlequins away on 8 June 2008. Warrington won 40–24.
Last game: Wakefield away on 27 February 2009. Warrington lost 48–22.

Verdict: Lowes was given the job after a good run as caretaker coach but that turned out to be a mistake. A great player with the Bradford Bulls and a capable assistant coach, but not cut out for the top job. He did not look or sound the part.

Tony Smith (2009–)
Played: 95
Won: 67   71 per cent
Drew: 0   0 per cent
Lost: 28   29 per cent
First game: Leeds home on 8 March 2009. Warrington lost 20–14.
Honours: Challenge Cup 2009 and 2010
League Leaders' Shield 2011

Verdict: Tony Smith proved to be the missing piece in the jigsaw. Building on the foundations laid by Paul Cullen and benefiting from the financial clout of Simon Moran, he has turned the Wolves into an awesome machine with a resolute defence and countless options in attack. Smith has brought new levels of professionalism to the club and so the back-to-back Challenge Cup wins may only be the start.

SUPER LEAGUE DREAM TEAM

This was introduced in 1996 and the following Warrington players have been selected:

1996	Paul Sculthorpe (second-row)
2003	Graham Appo (stand-off)
2005	Martin Gleeson (centre)
2007	Kevin Penny (wing)
2008	Ben Westwood (second row)
2009	Adrian Morley (prop)
2010	Matt King (centre), Morley (prop), Westwood (second row)
2011	Joel Monaghan (wing), Garreth Carvell (prop), Westwood (second row)

LOVE MATCH

Warrington supporters John Prior and Patricia Thompson had their marriage blessed on the pitch before the home game against Castleford at Wilderspool in August 1999. John told me last year that, to complete a wonderful day, Warrington won. Sadly, the records show that Warrington actually lost 8–6. Both John and Patricia now work for the club.

SMOKING HOT

Imperial Tobacco sponsored an annual knockout competition, under various titles – Player's No. 6 Trophy, John Player Trophy, Regal Trophy – for 25 seasons from 1971/72 and Warrington won it four times.

1974   Warrington 27–16 Rochdale Hornets
1978   Warrington 9–4 Widnes
1981   Warrington 12–5 Barrow
1991   Warrington 12–2 Bradford Northern

FASTEST SENDING OFF

Warrington captain Adrian Morley must be sick of being asked about this but, in 2003, he was sent off after just 7 seconds of the first Test between Great Britain and Australia at the JJB Stadium. Morley, who was playing for the Sydney Roosters at the time, was shown the red card by referee Steve Ganson for a high tackle on Robbie Kearns. The depleted GB side put on a brave performance before losing 22–18.

FURTHER READING

Last of the Dinosaurs, The Kevin Ashcroft Story, by Maurice Bamford (2008)

The Great Bev, The rugby league career of Brian Bevan, by Robert Gate (2002)

Pint Size: Andy Gregory – Heroes and Hangovers, with Phil Thomas (2000)

Biting Back, The Mike Gregory Story, with Erica Gregory and Dave Hadfield (2006)

Iestyn Harris: There and Back (2006)

Saint and Sinner, by Alex Murphy OBE (2000)

Sculthorpe: Man of Steel (2007)